PIANO / VOCAL / GUITAR

ISBN 978-1-4950-0687-6

7777 W. Bluemound Rd. P.O. Box 13819 Milwaukee, WI 53213

In Australia Contact:
Hal Leonard Australia Pty. Ltd.
4 Lentara Court
Cheltenham, Victoria, 3192 Australia
Email: ausadmin@halleonard.com.au

Visit Hal Leonard Online at
www.halleonard.com

DETROIT MADE

Words and Music by
JOHN HIATT

D/A
A5
Came up from the coun - try, ba - by; cit - y's where I stay.
Chrome that takes the moon - light on sea to shin - ing sea.

Got me a deuce and a quar - ter, ba - by; that's all
You can hear those glass packs rum - ble to the

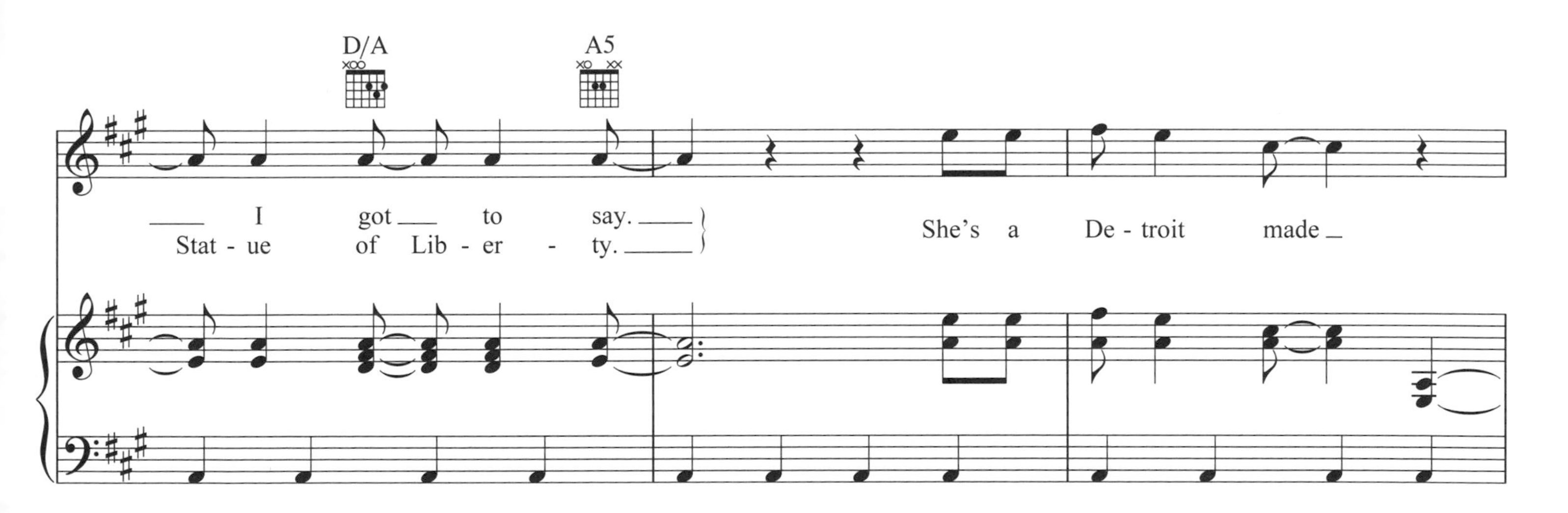
D/A
A5
I got to say.
Stat - ue of Lib - er - ty.
She's a De - troit made

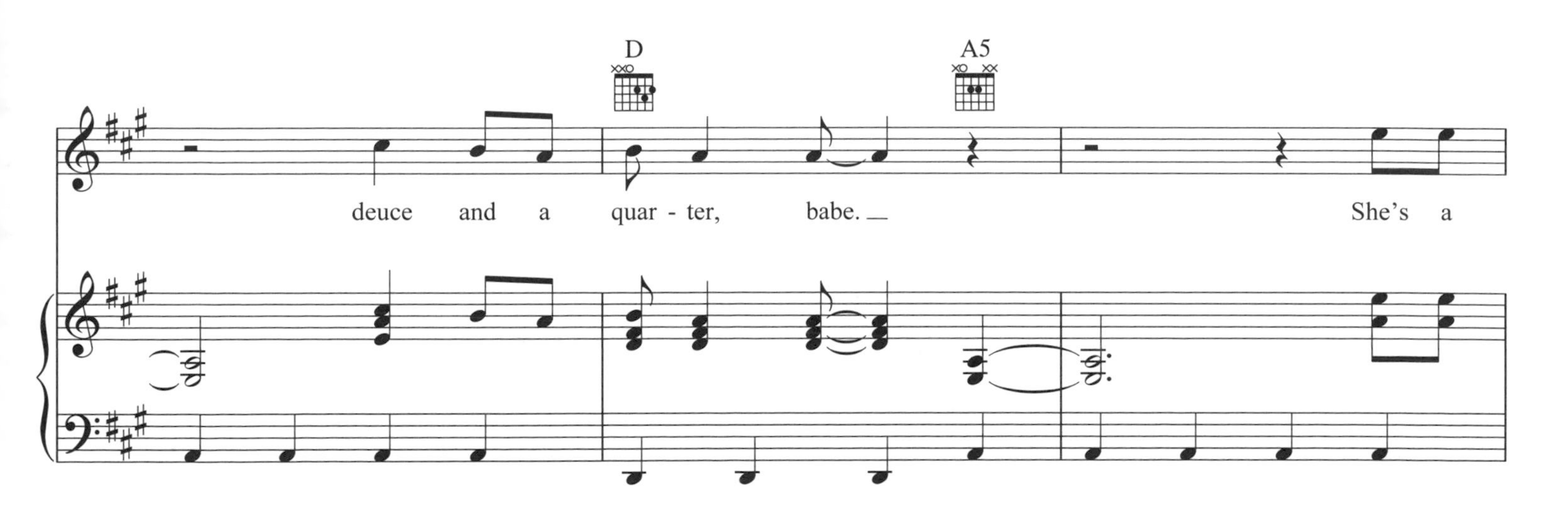
D
A5
deuce and a quar - ter, babe.
She's a

D
A5
De - troit made
deuce and a quar - ter, babe.

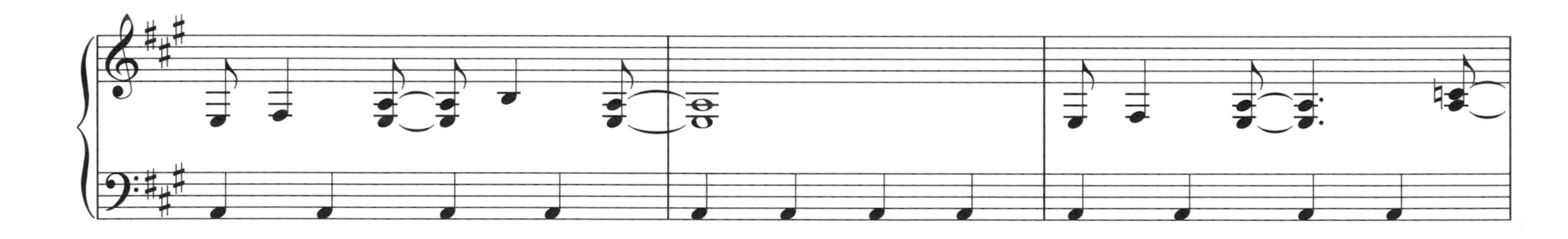

Now,

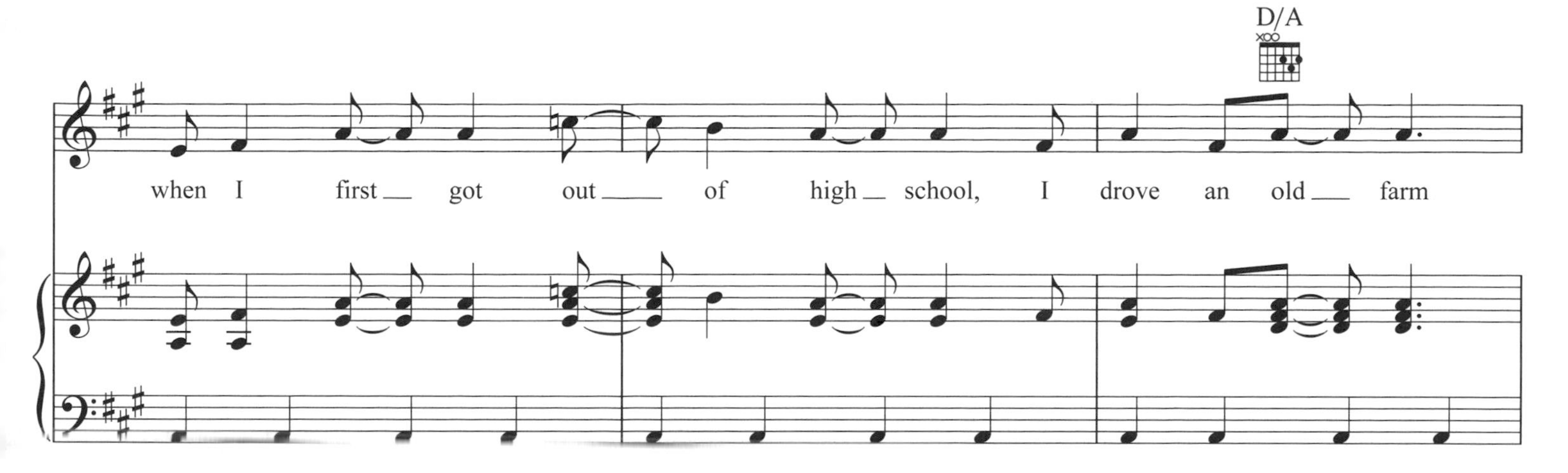
D/A
when I first got out of high school, I drove an old farm

A5
truck. Well, all the girls, they walked right by me, did-

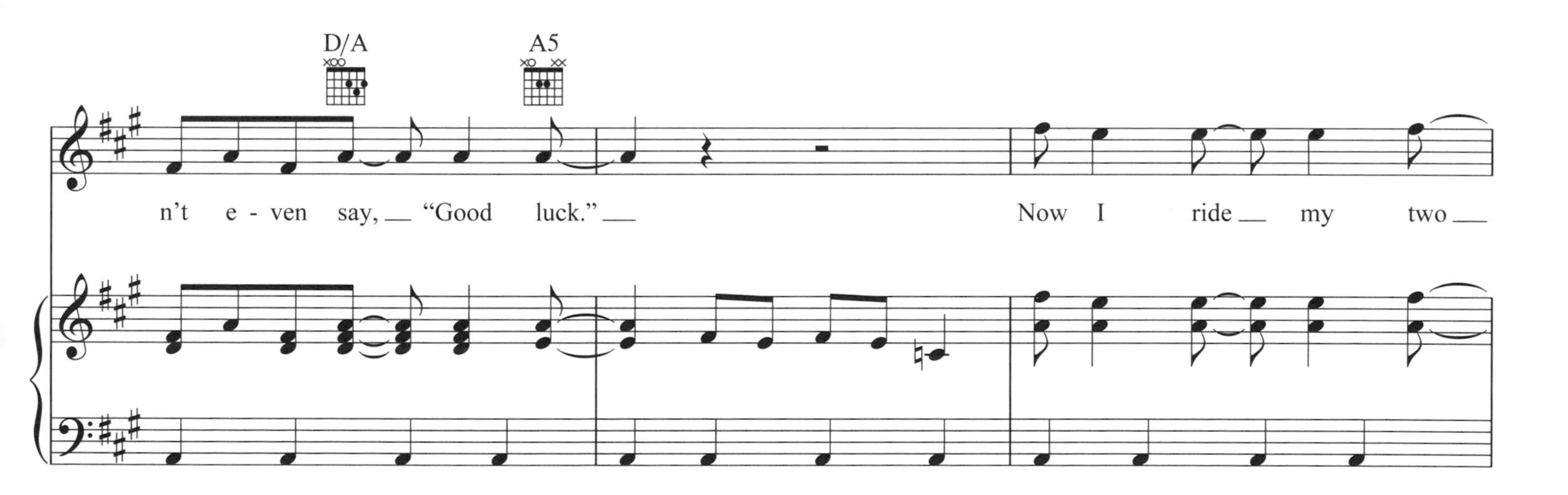
D/A
A5
n't e-ven say, "Good luck." Now I ride my two

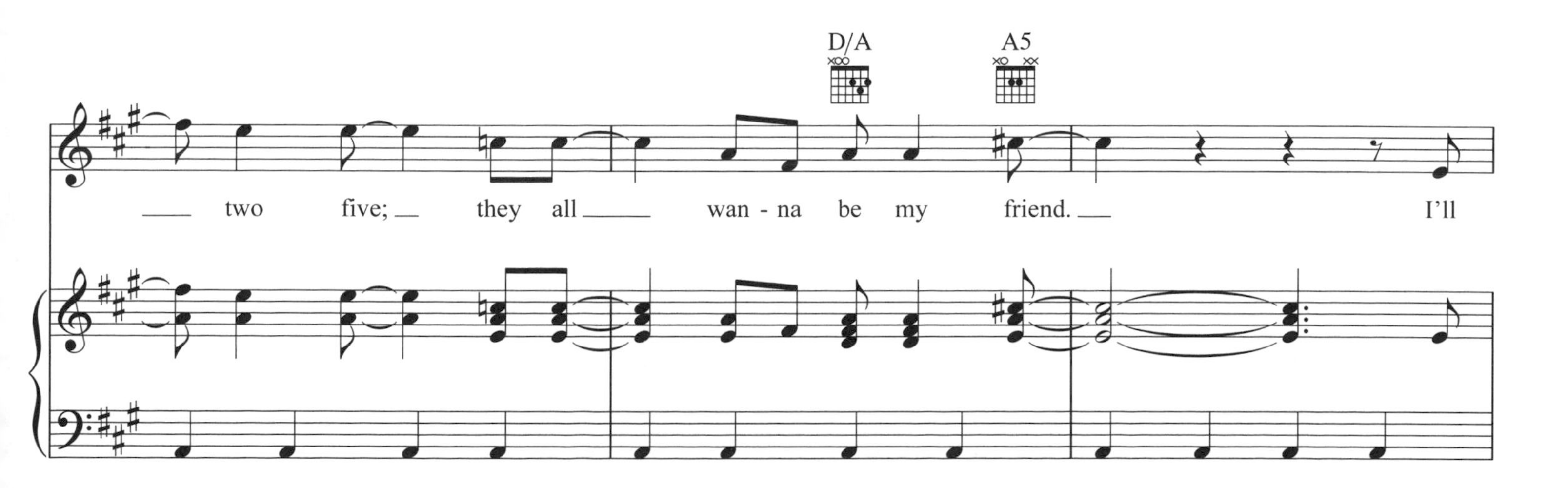
D/A
A5
two five; they all wan-na be my friend. I'll

D/A
A5
pick you up lat - er to - night, now, ba - by, if you can wait 'til then.

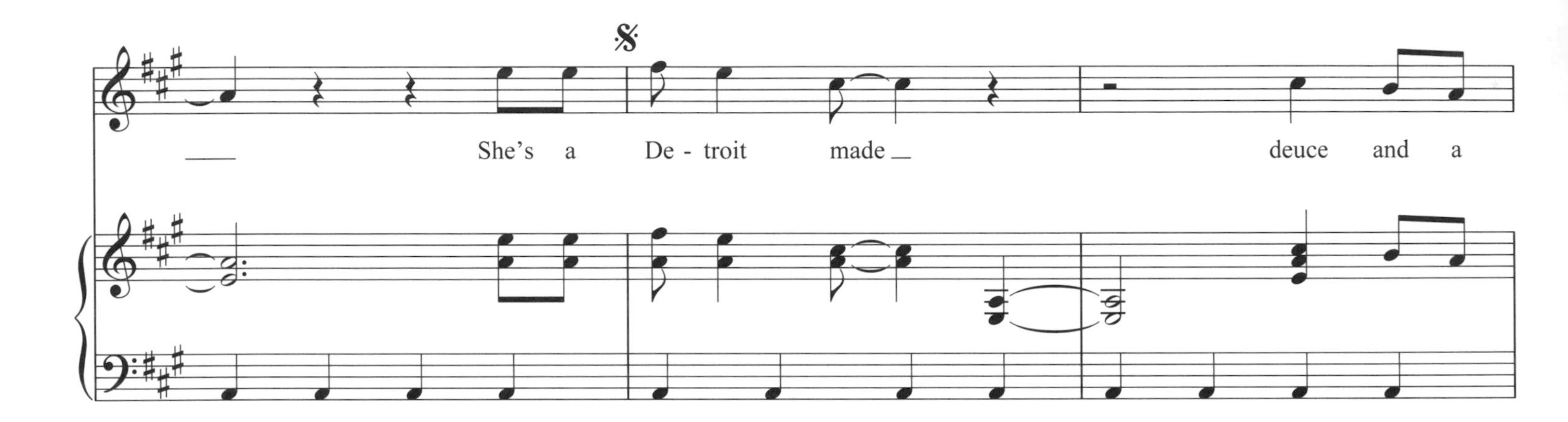
She's a De - troit made
deuce and a

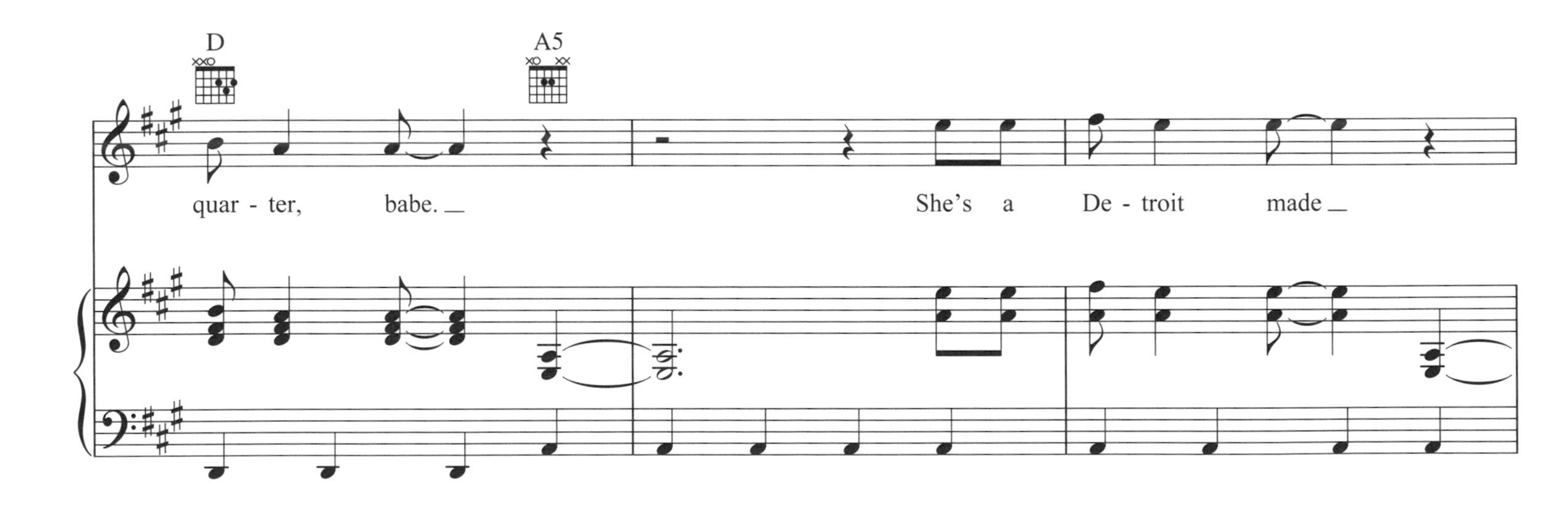
D
A5
quar - ter, babe.
She's a De - troit made

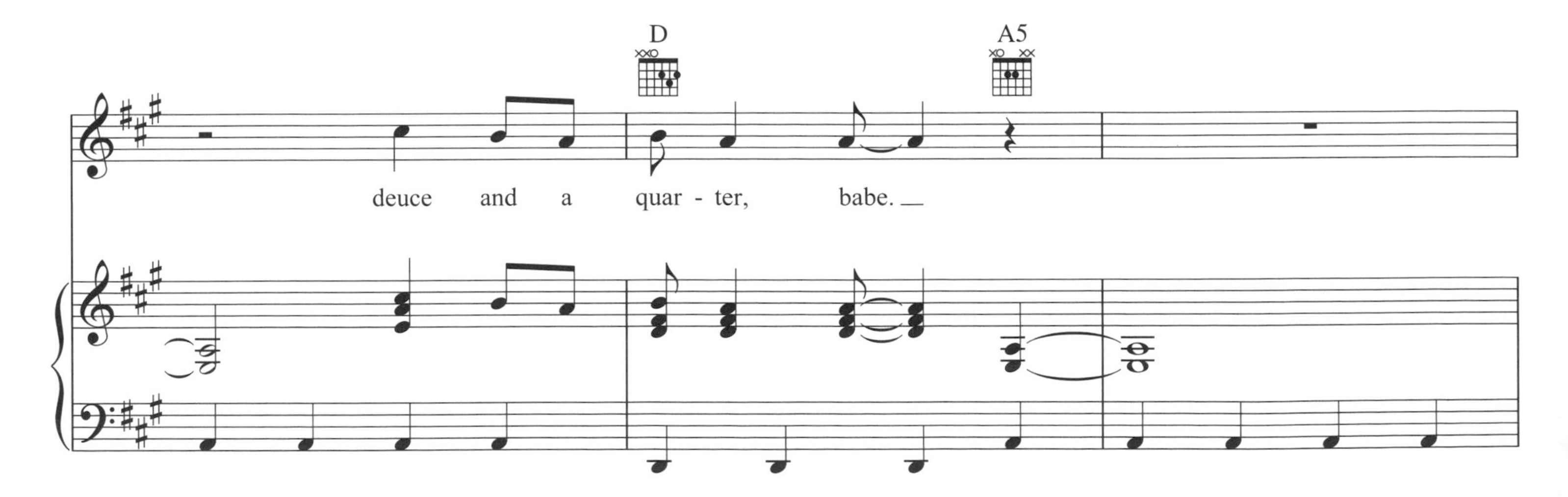
D
A5
deuce and a quar - ter, babe.

D
A5
De - troit made
deuce and a quar - ter, babe.
De - troit made
deuce and a
D
A5
To Coda
A5
quar - ter, babe.
(Instrumental solo ad lib.)

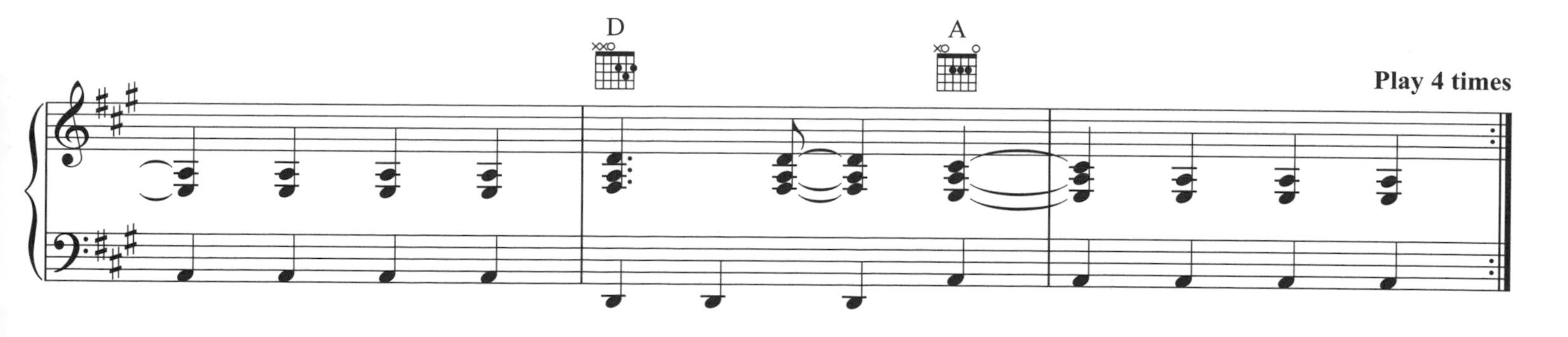
D
A
Play 4 times

D/A
A5
Just a - bout ev - 'ry cat I know wants him a Coupe de Ville.

I pay half the price, I get twice as nice and they still

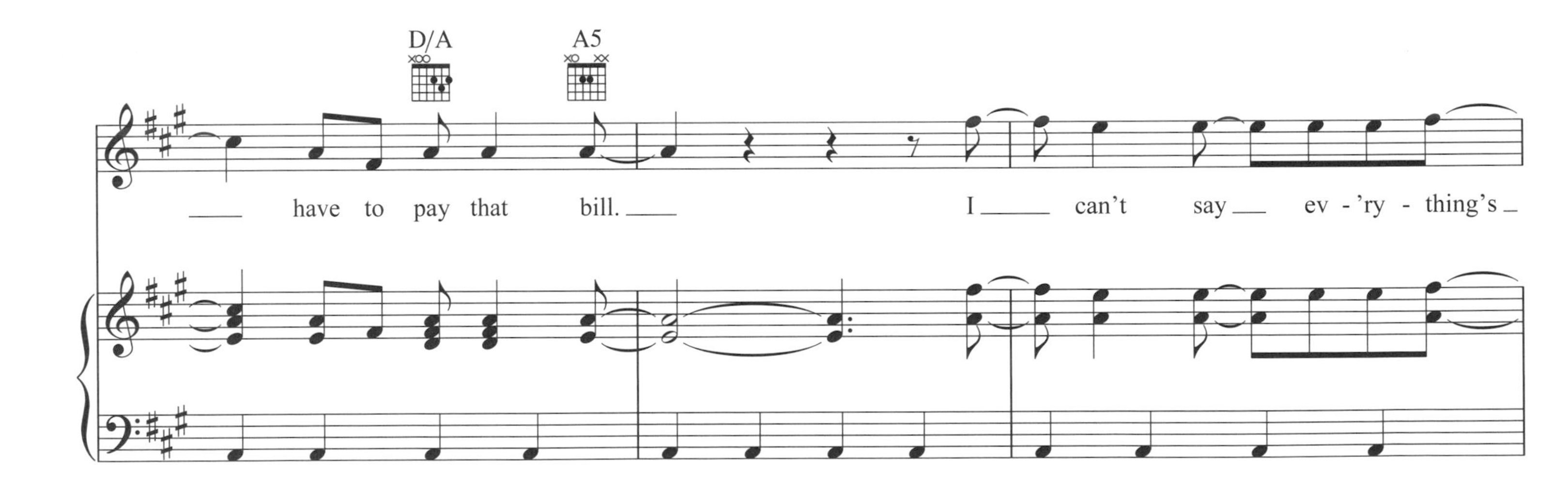
D/A
A5
have to pay that bill. I can't say ev - 'ry - thing's

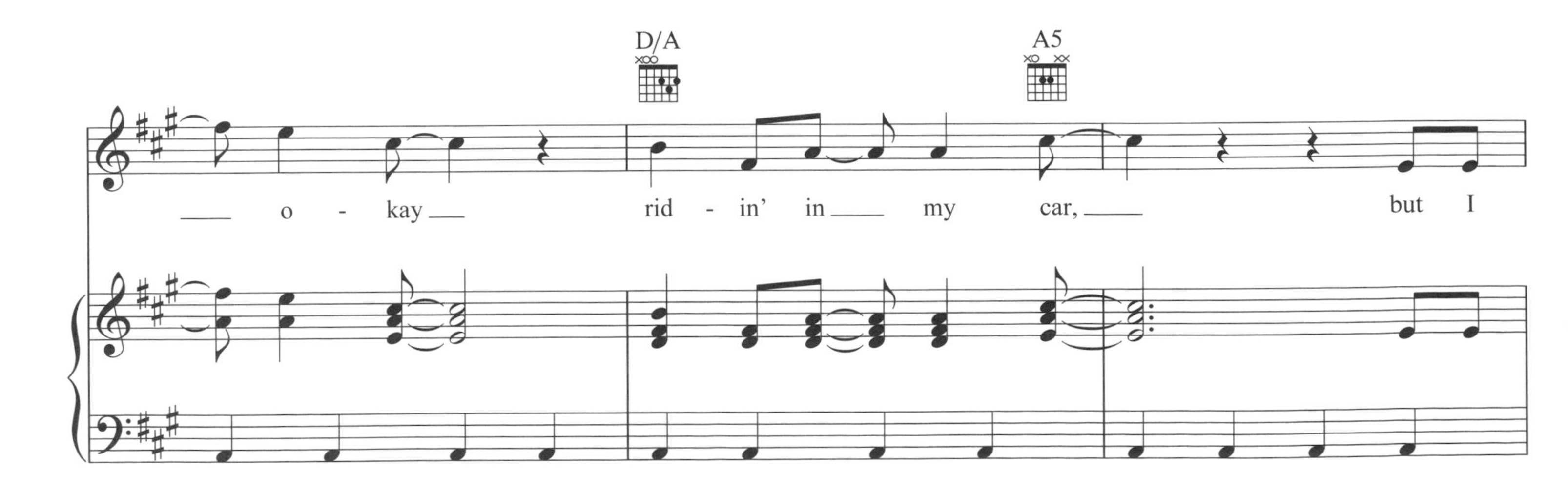
D/A
A5
o - kay rid - in' in my car, but I

D/A
A5
got me a deuce and a quar - ter, ba - by; she goes like a shoot - ing star.

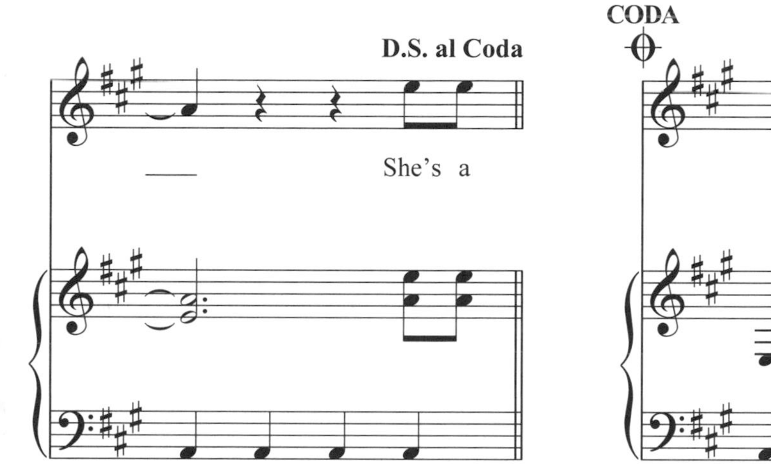
D.S. al Coda
She's a

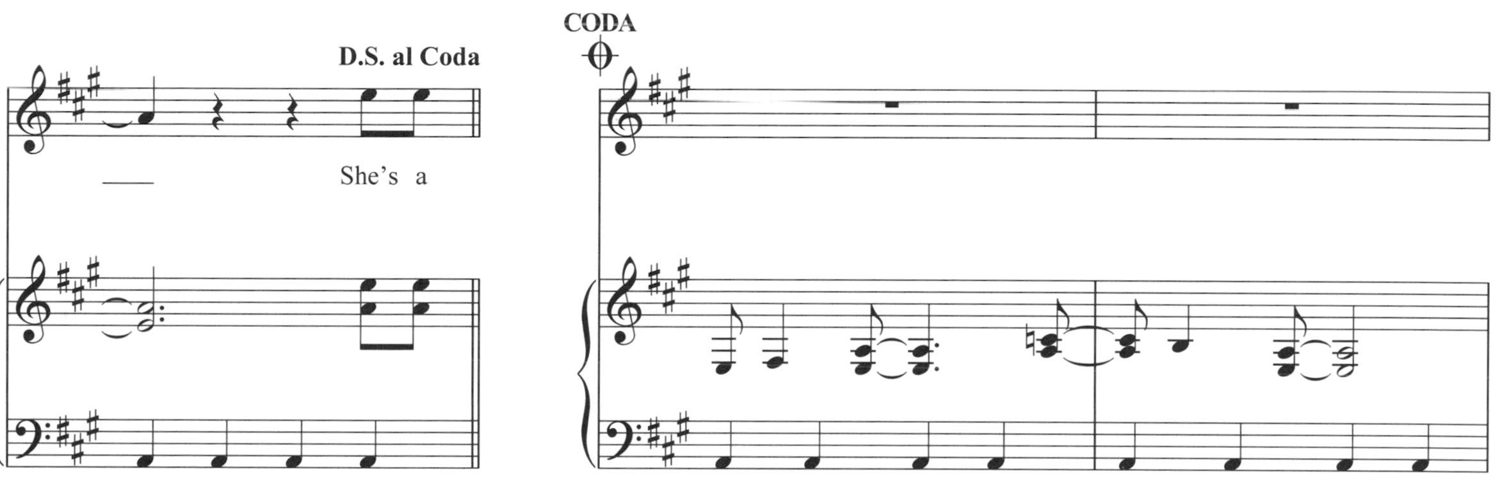
CODA

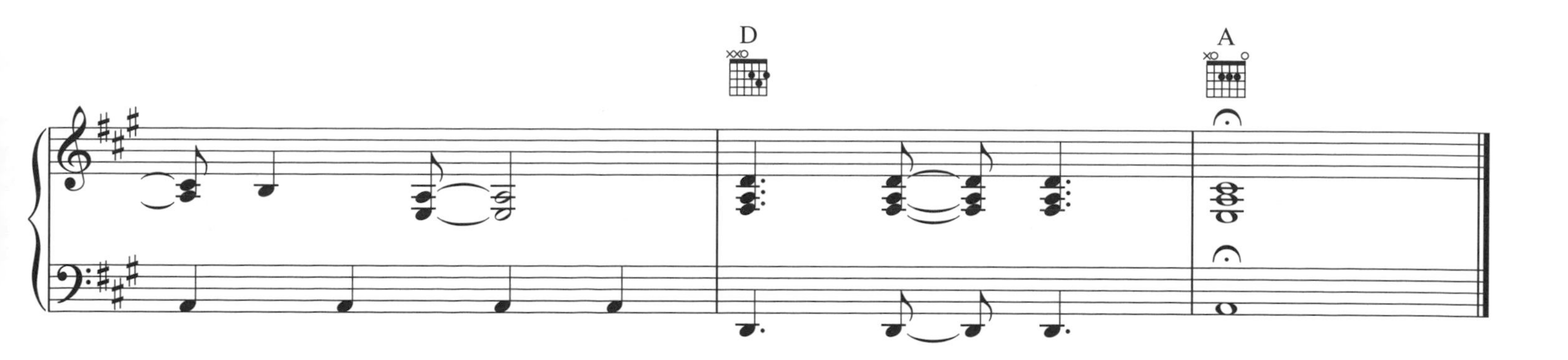
D
A

HEY GYPSY

Words and Music by
BOB SEGER

* *Guitar is tuned to D on recording. Chord frames are provided here in standard tuning.*

To Coda
A7
G7
I am tired of this wait - in', I ain't gon - na wait no more.
Let's head on home, I'll give you your fa - vor - ite toy.
You can treat me bad, ma - ma, you'll
D7
1
2
Hey ma -
We've been
all o - ver town,
chas - in' the crowds.
I'm get - tin' kind - a nerv - ous 'cause the
mu - sic's too loud.
Hey gyp - sy,
G7
where we gon - na

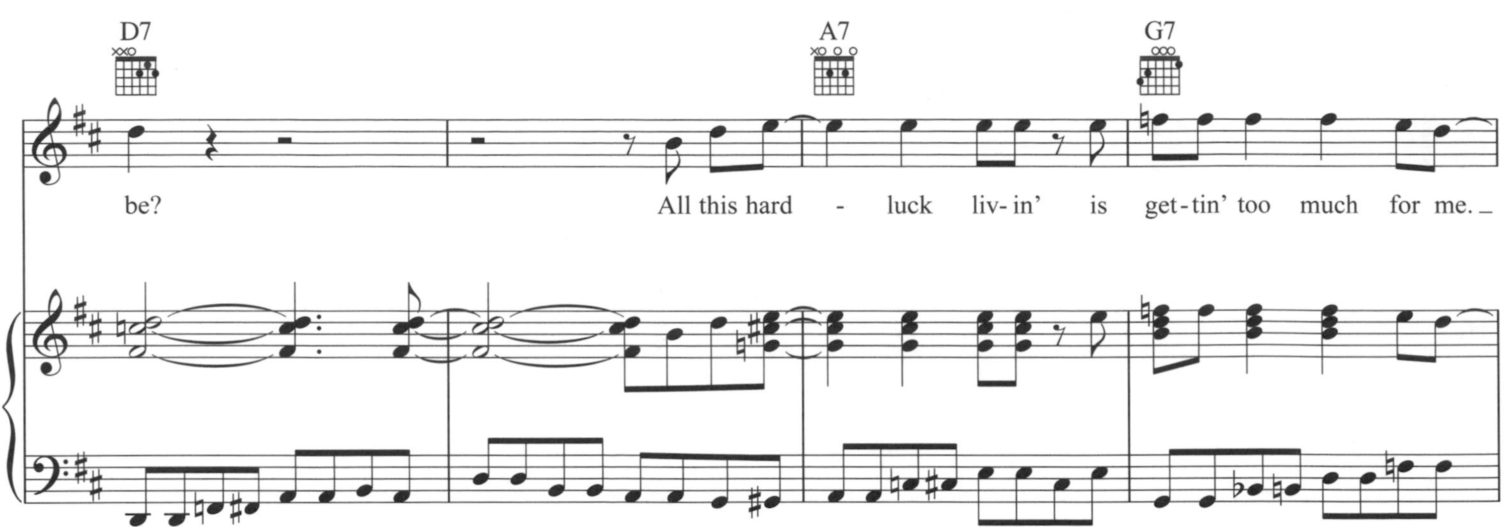
D7
A7
G7
be?
All this hard - luck liv- in' is get- tin' too much for me.

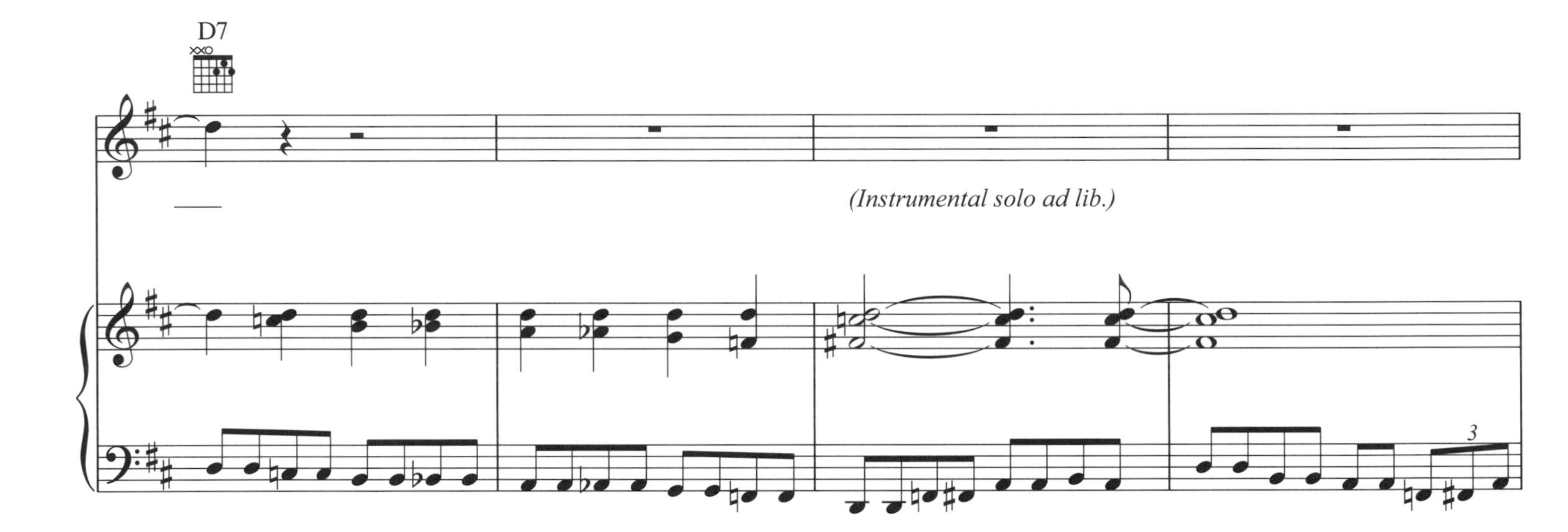
D7
(Instrumental solo ad lib.)
3

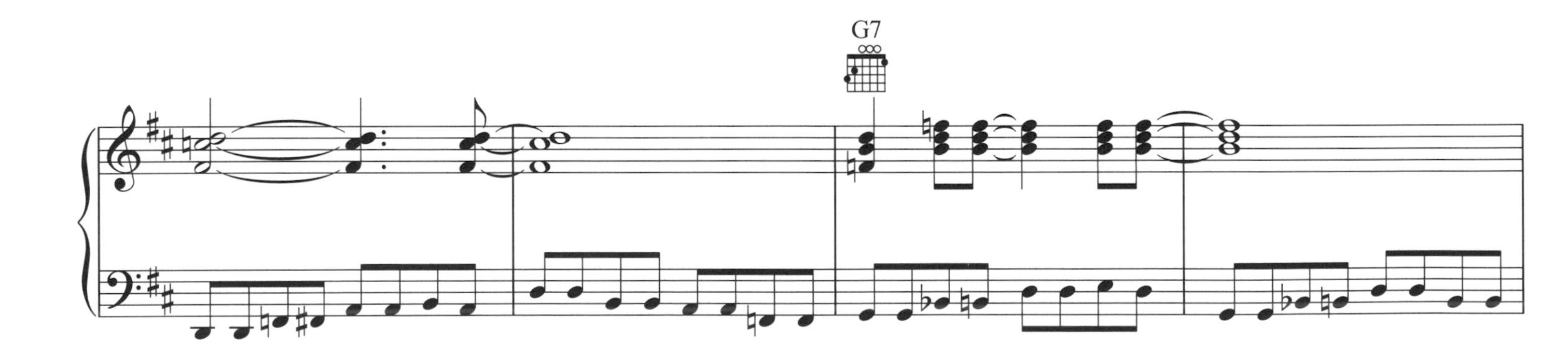
G7

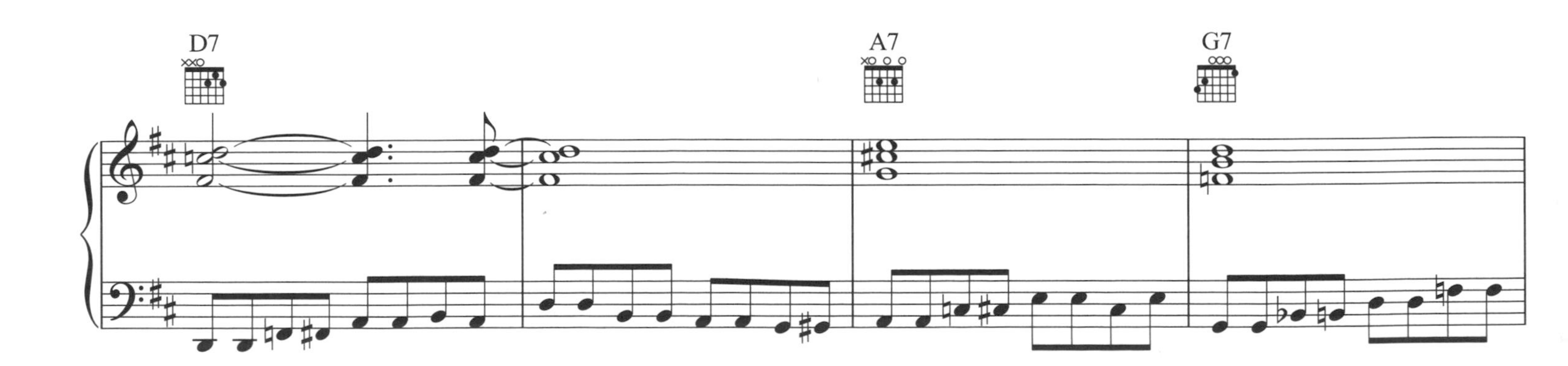
D7
A7
G7

D7
G7
D7
Keep on push-in' me a-round the clock. I

G7
D7
G7
keep on fall-in' and I can't get up. You know I love you, but e-

D7
E7
A7♯5
D.S. al Coda
nough's e-nough. You move too fast, girl, you play too rough. Hey gyp-

CODA
G7
N.C.
E♭7
D7
nev-er get an-oth-er a-gain.

THE DEVIL'S RIGHT HAND

Words and Music by
STEVE EARLE

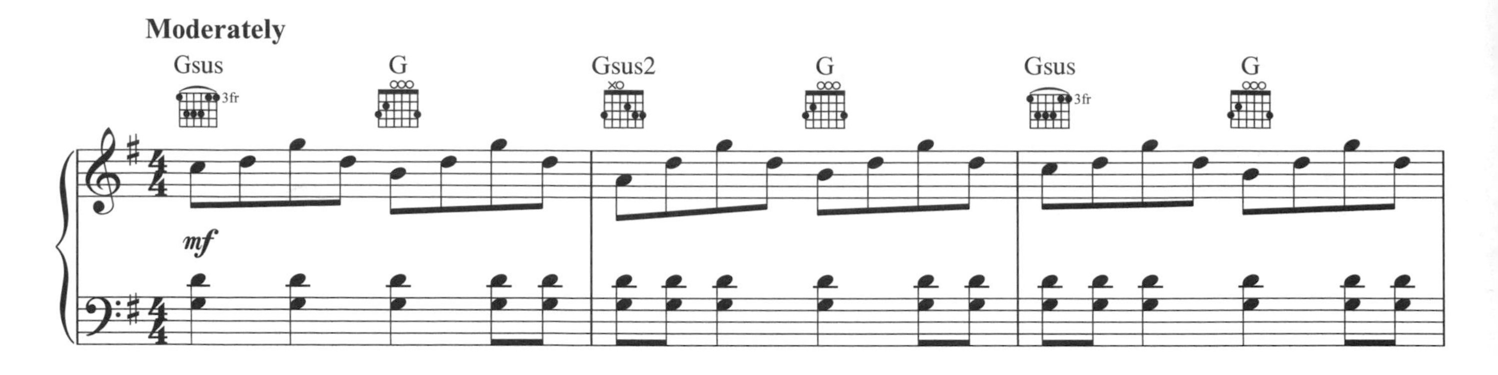

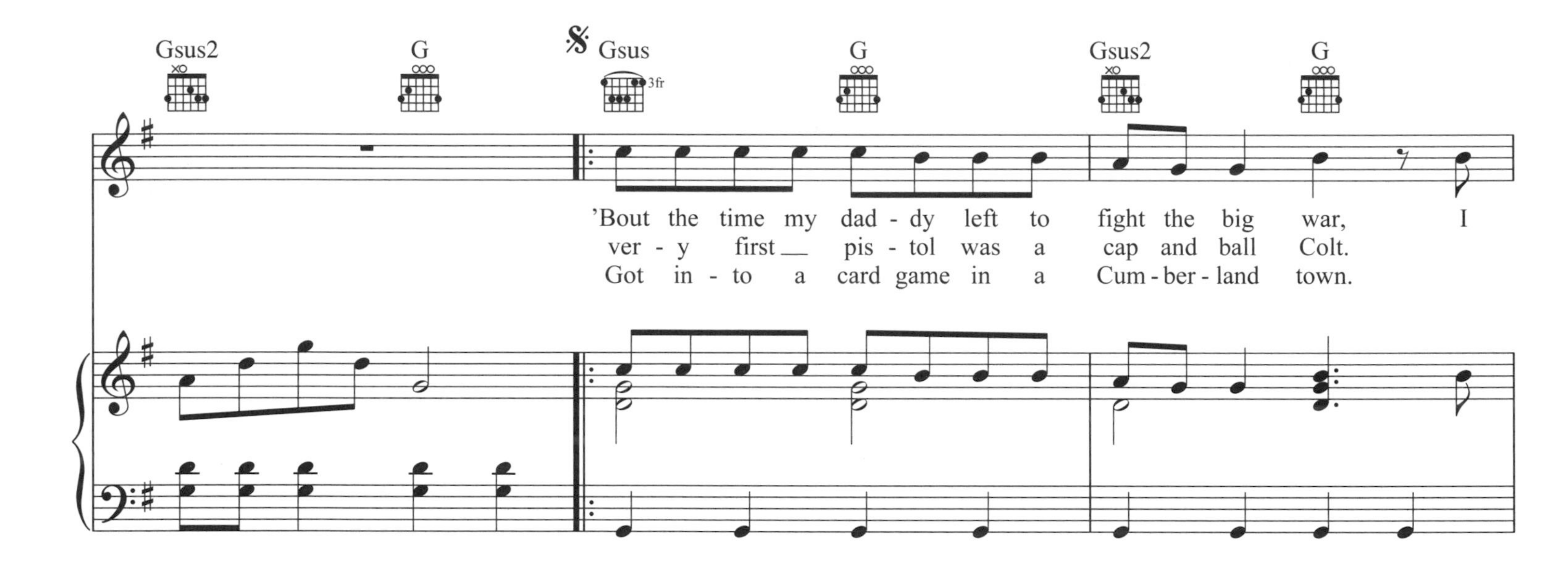

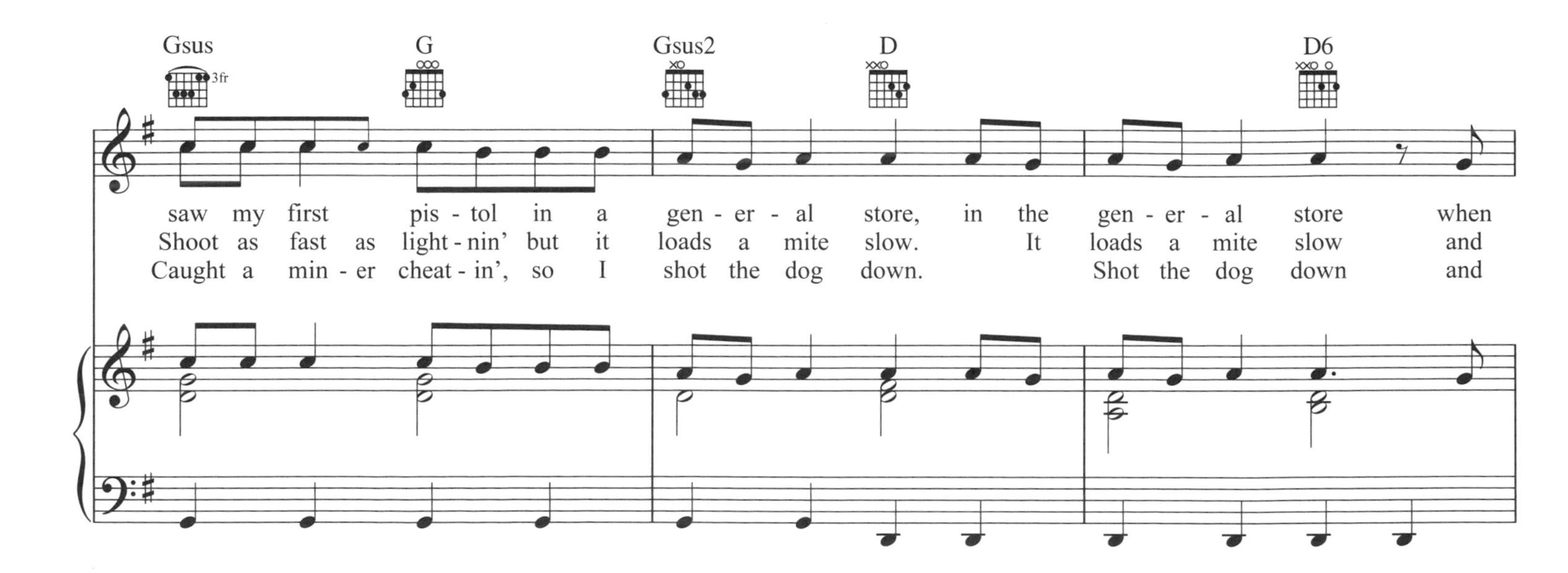

D
D6
D7
D6
G
I was thir - teen. I thought it was the fin - est thing I ev - er had seen. So I
soon I found out it - 'll get you in - to trou - ble, but it can't_ get you out. 'Bout_
watched the man fall. Nev - er touched his hol - ster, nev - er had a chance to draw. Trial_

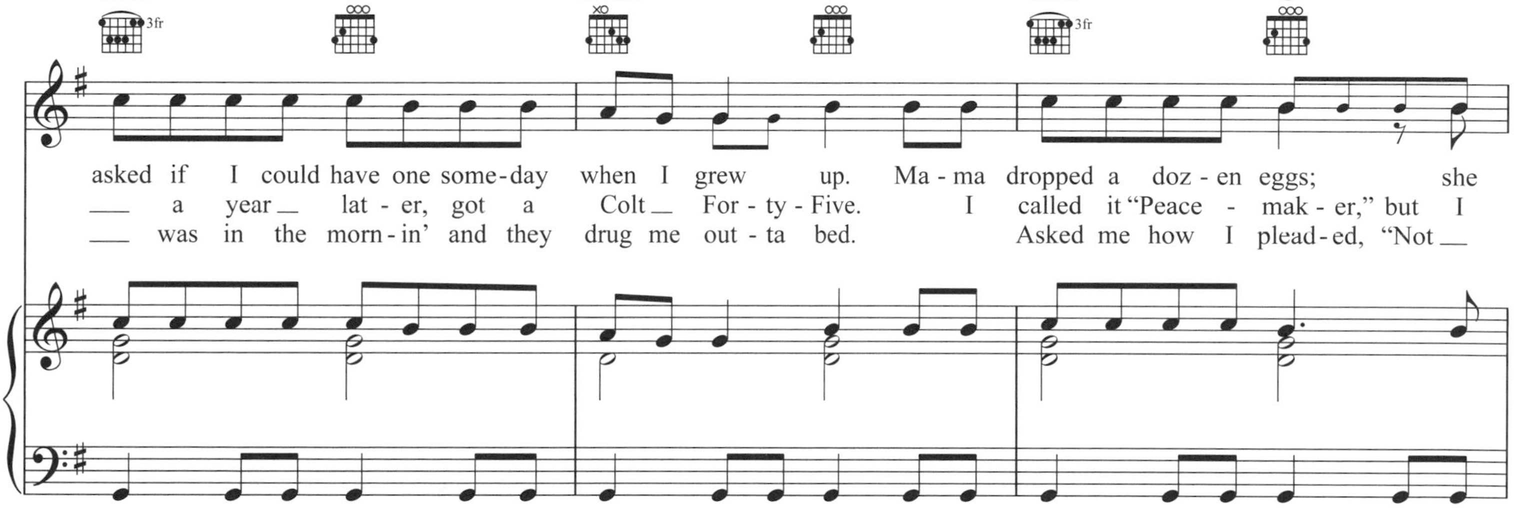
Gsus
3fr
G
Gsus2
G
Gsus
3fr
G
asked if I could have one some-day when I grew up. Ma - ma dropped a doz - en eggs; she
___ a year_ lat - er, got a Colt_ For - ty - Five. I called it "Peace - mak - er," but I
___ was in the morn - in' and they drug me out - ta bed. Asked me how I plead - ed, "Not_

Gsus2
D
D6
D
D6
real - ly blew_ up. She real - ly blew up, she did - n't un - der - stand.
nev - er knew_ why. I nev - er knew why, I did - n't un - der - stand.
guilt - y," I ___ said. "Not guilt - y," I said. "You got the wrong man.

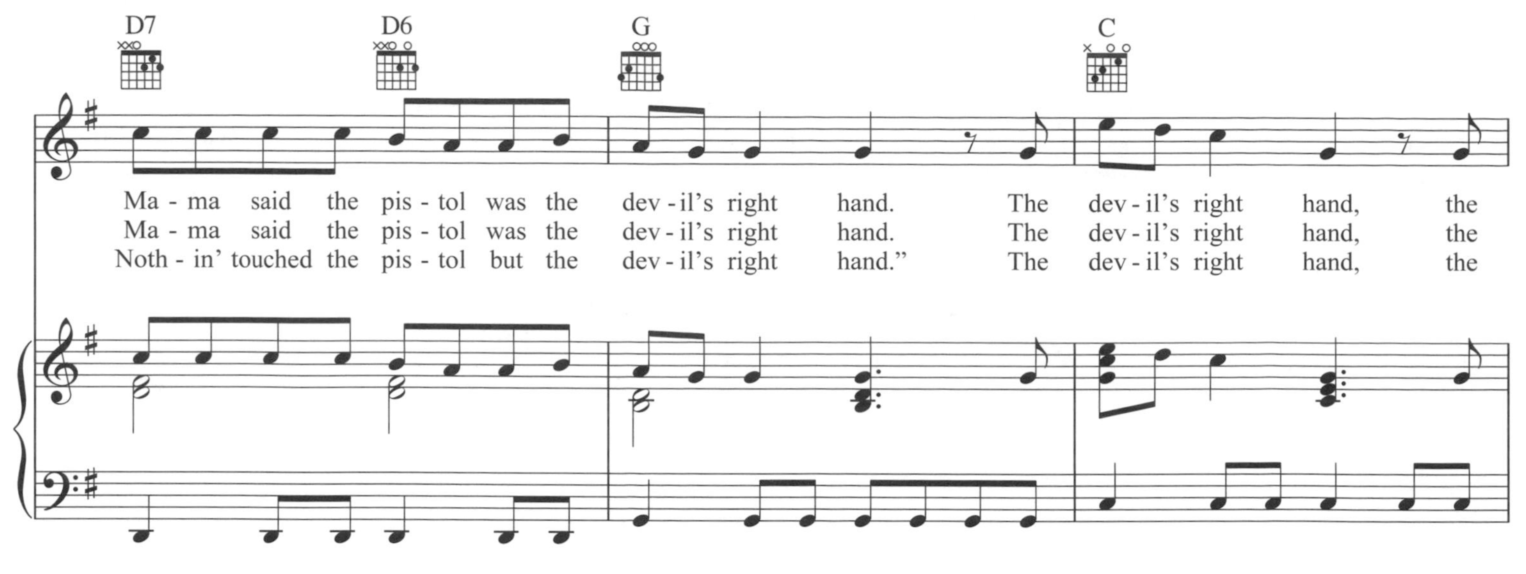
D7
D6
G
C
Ma - ma said the pis - tol was the dev - il's right hand. The dev - il's right hand, the
Ma - ma said the pis - tol was the dev - il's right hand. The dev - il's right hand, the
Noth - in' touched the pis - tol but the dev - il's right hand." The dev - il's right hand, the

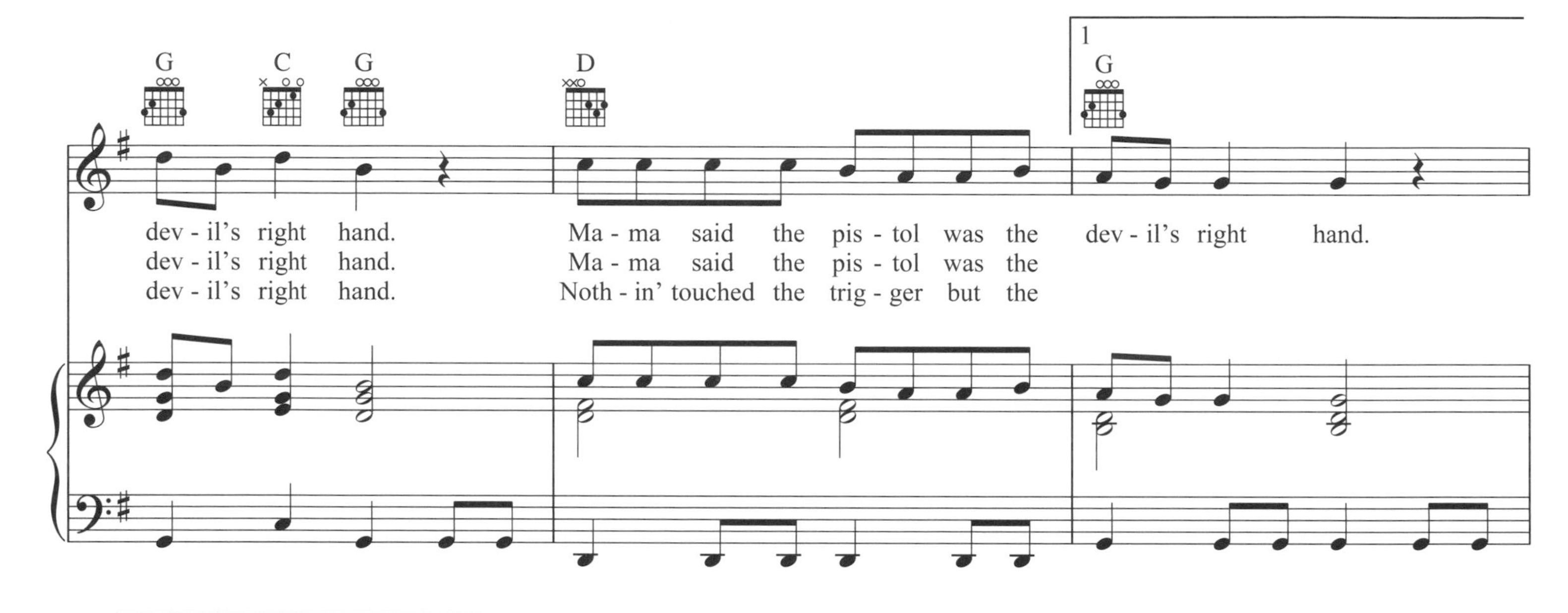
1
G
C
G
D
G
dev - il's right hand. Ma - ma said the pis - tol was the dev - il's right hand.
dev - il's right hand. Ma - ma said the pis - tol was the
dev - il's right hand. Noth - in' touched the trig - ger but the

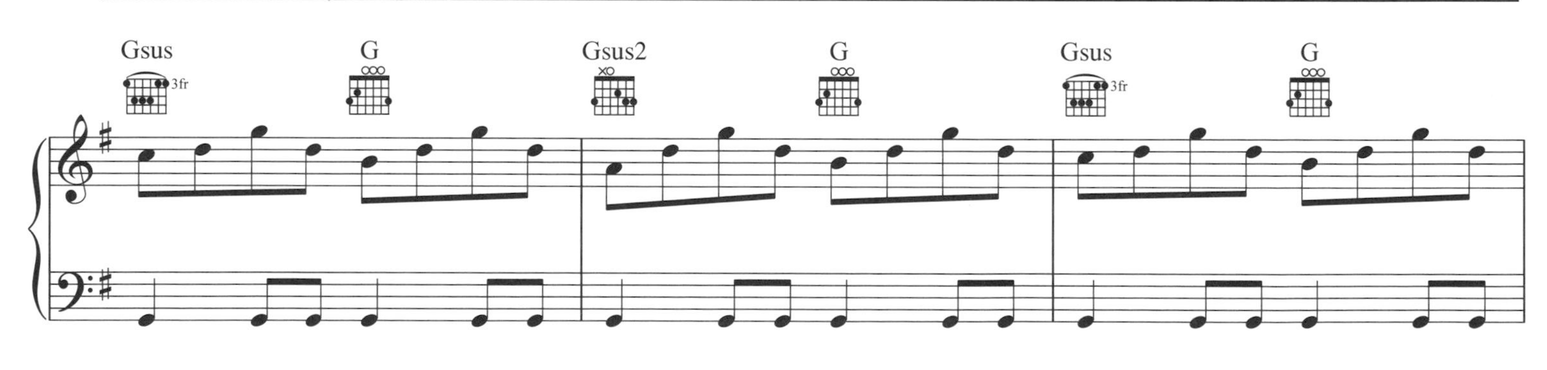
Gsus
3fr
G
Gsus2
G
Gsus
3fr
G

2, 3
Gsus2
G
G
C
My dev - il's right hand.
dev - il's right hand.
The dev - il's right hand, the

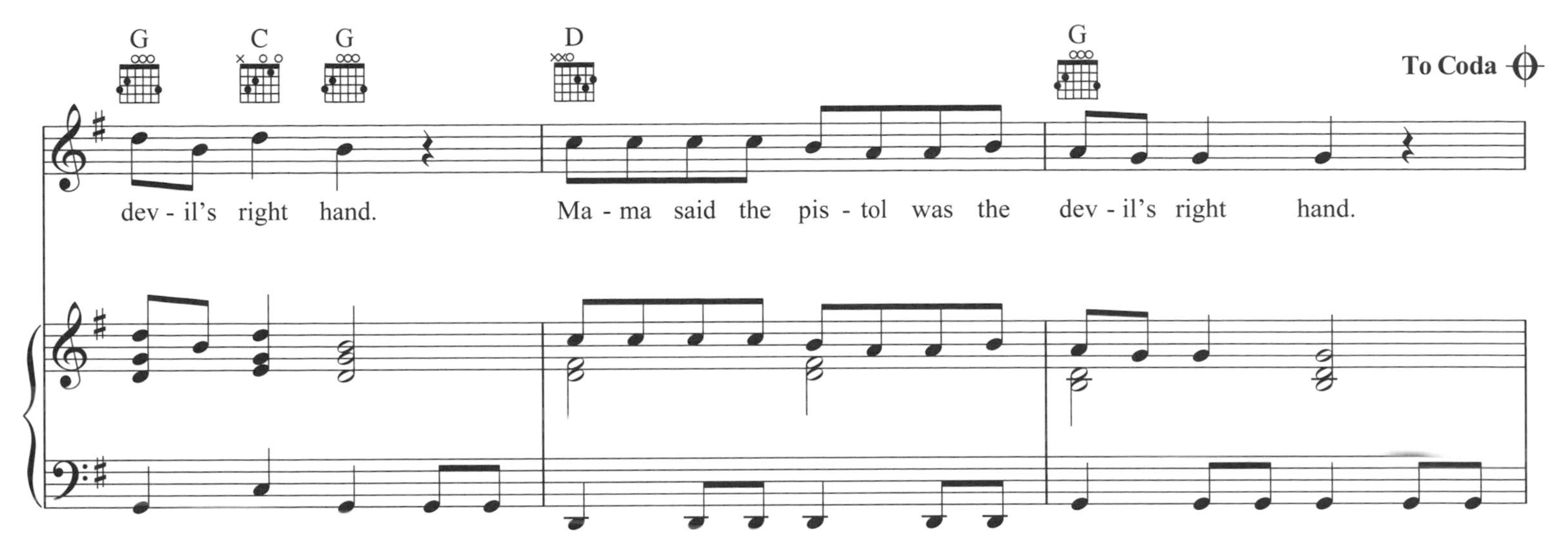
G
C
G
D
G
To Coda
dev - il's right hand.
Ma - ma said the pis - tol was the
dev - il's right hand.

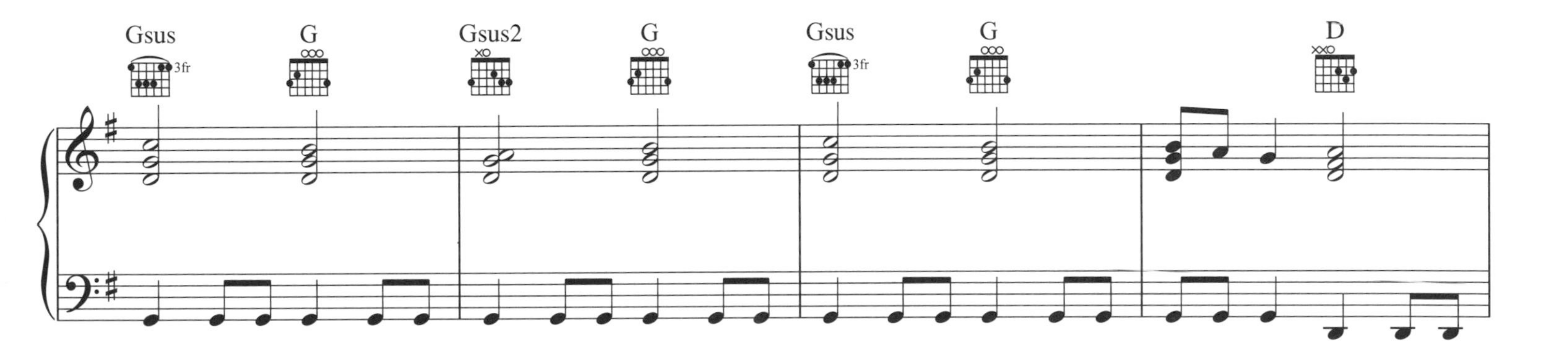
Gsus
3fr
G
Gsus2
G
Gsus
3fr
G
D

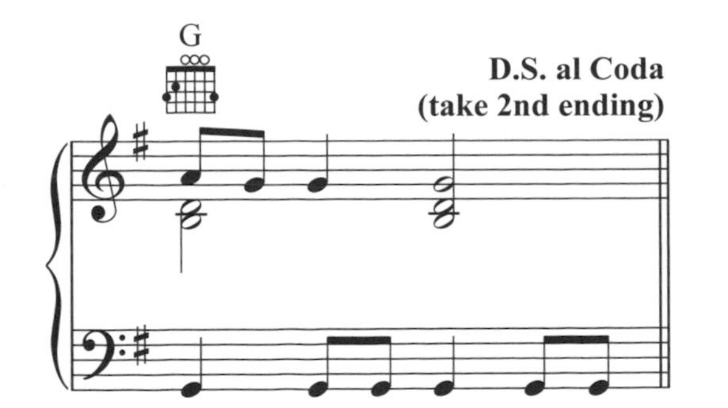
G
D.S. al Coda
(take 2nd ending)

CODA
N.C.
G5
3fr

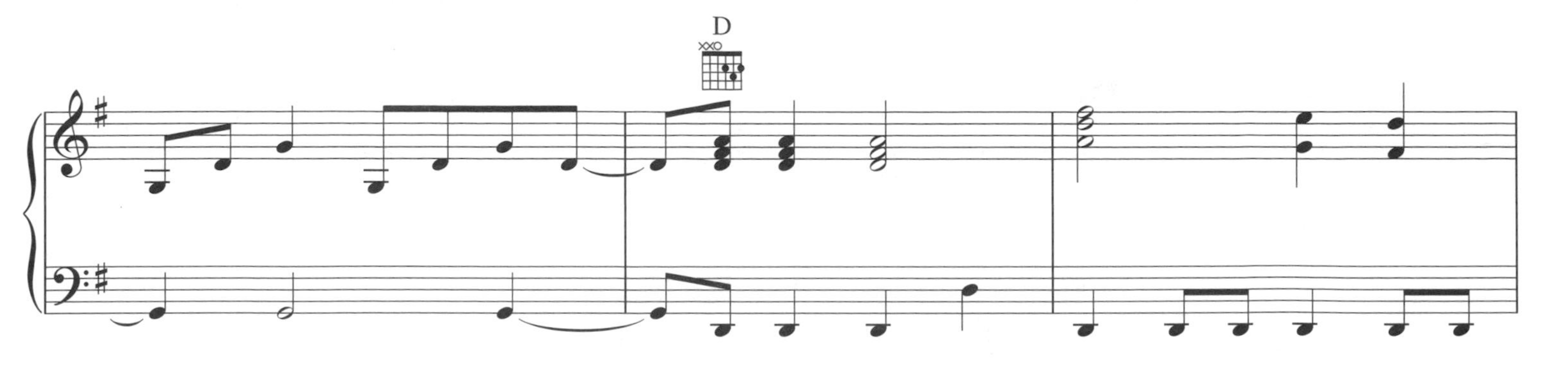
D

G

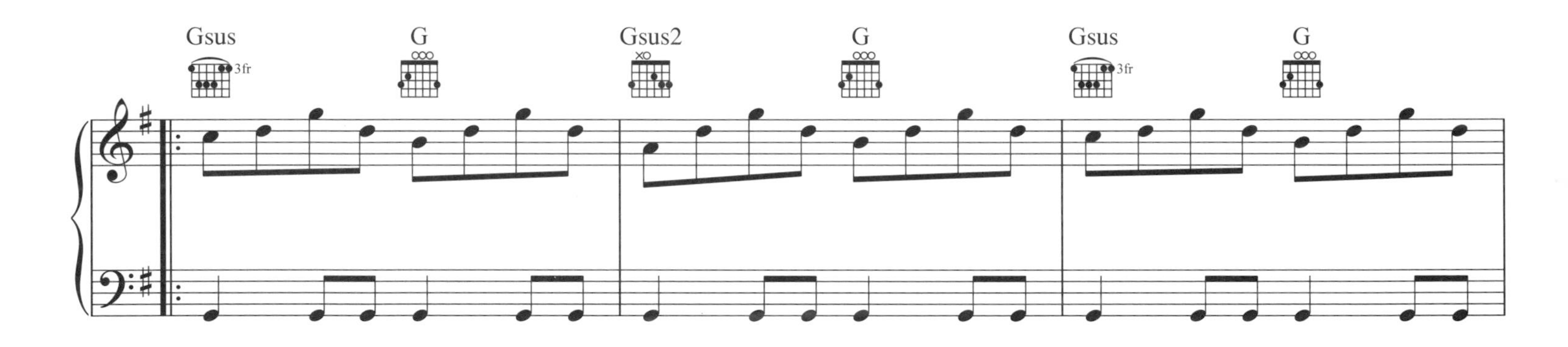
Gsus
3fr
G
Gsus2
G
Gsus
3fr
G

D

Repeat and Fade
G
Optional Ending
G

EXIT

RIDE OUT

Words and Music by
BOB SEGER

* Recorded a half step lower.

lu - sions and de - lu - sions lead us where we should - n't go. Time to
world ___ will be watch - ing; there's a crack in ev - 'ry lie. When it
dis - con - nect from clut - ter, time ___ to hit the road. Ride out ___ to a
o - pens like a cha - sm, you can kiss it all good - bye. Ride out ___ to the
bold new ho - ri - zon, where the sun may be shin - in' on a place you've nev - er seen. Ride out, _
high cop - per can - yons, past the shacks and the man - sions where the riv - ers nev - er end. Ride out, _

To Coda
___ lift your soul and your spir - it. Take a chance and get near it; ev - 'ry -
___ past the peaks and the me - sas, to the wide o - pen spac - es you may

bod - y needs a dream. Is the me - di - a for real? Do we fake or do we feel? Do we
base all our ap - peal on a mod - el or a myth? It's a mar - ket cor - rec - tion, it's ad -
dic - tion res - ur - rec - tion. It's the last thing you men - tion be - fore you knock it stiff. Ride out
where the hills meet the val - leys, far from cam - paigns and ral - lies and the

things we do for oil. Ride out.
It's the real and i - mag-ined with the

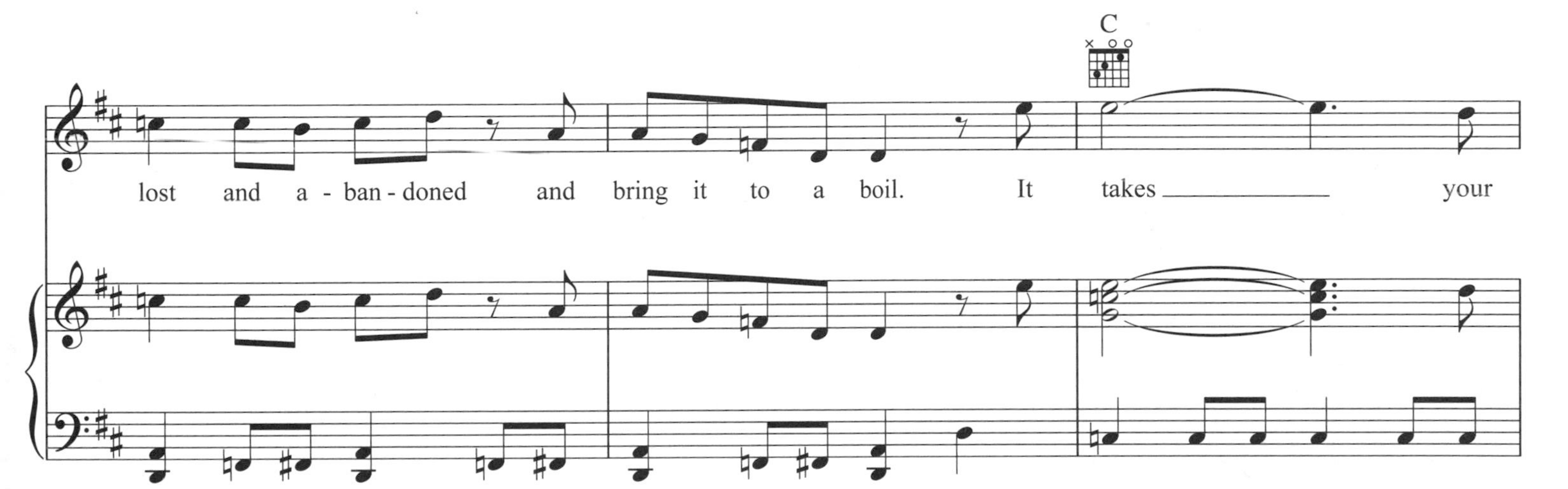
C
lost and a - ban - doned and bring it to a boil. It takes your

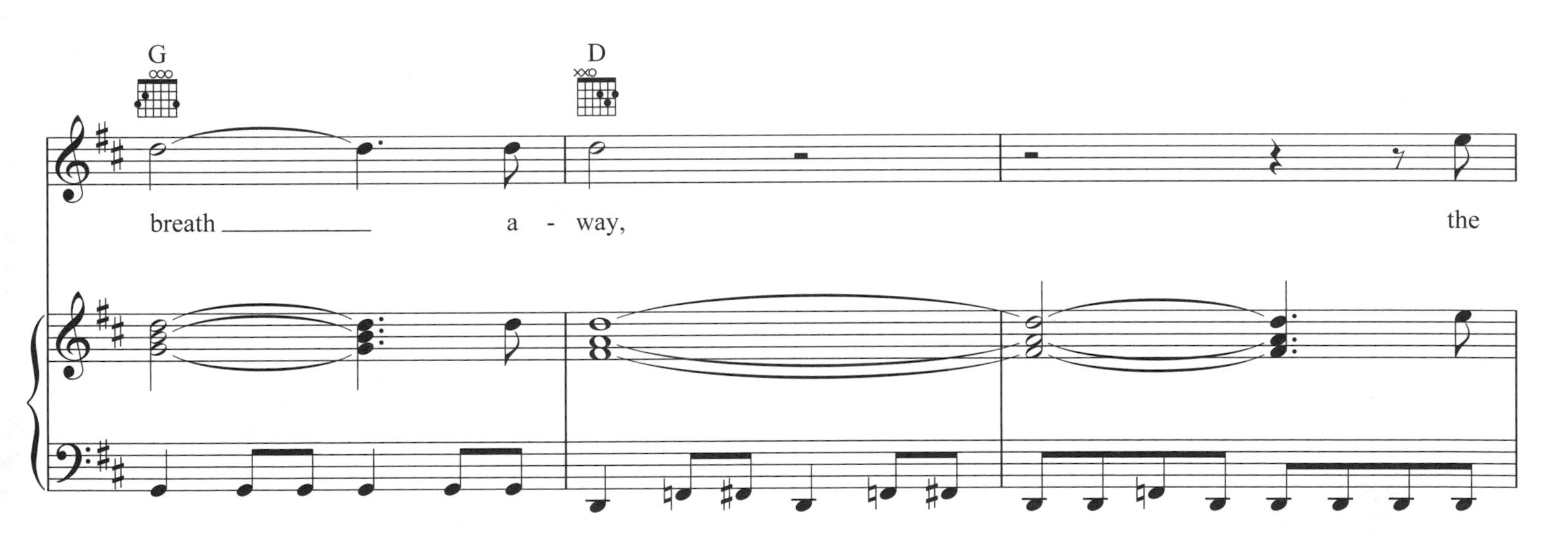
G
D
breath a - way, the

C
G
F5
way we pay and pay, (pay) and

E5
D5
5fr
pay (and pay) and pay.
(Vocal 1st time only)
1
2
D.S. al Coda
You can
CODA
nev - er see a - gain. Ride out
to a
brand - new ho - ri - zon, where the sun may be shin - in' on a place you've nev - er seen. Ride out,

lift your soul, lift your spir - it. Take a chance and get near it; ev - 'ry -
bod - y needs a dream. Ride out.
Play 3 times
Ride out.

ADAM AND EVE

Words and Music by KASEY CHAMBERS
and SHANE NICHOLSON

E
Am
say, but He was rest - in' on that sev - enth day. She met a

E
ser - pent that af - ter - noon. He smiled at her and she broke _ the

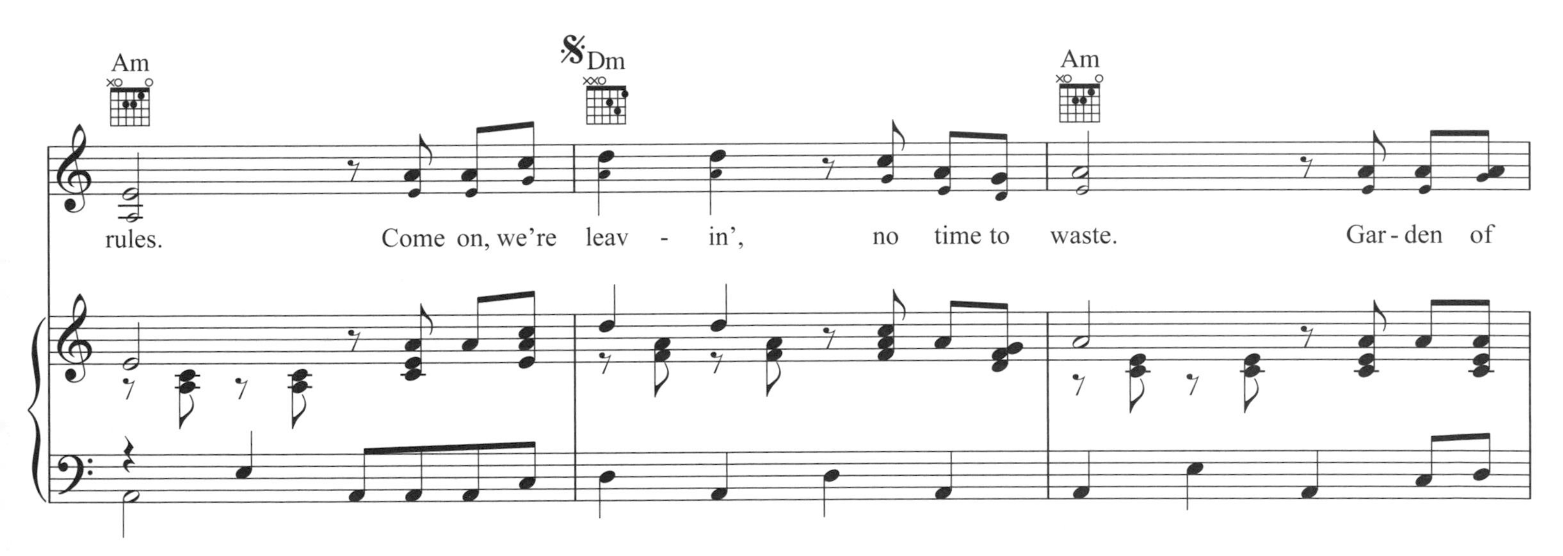
Am
Dm
Am
rules. Come on, we're leav - in', no time to waste. Gar - den of

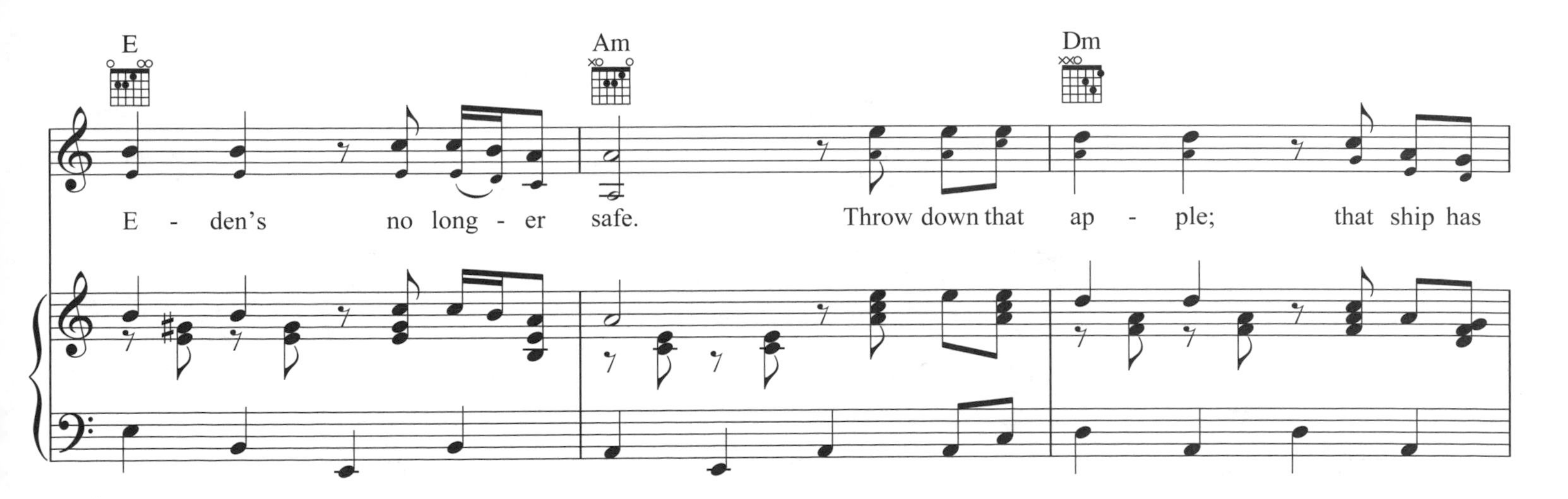
E
Am
Dm
E - den's no long - er safe. Throw down that ap - ple; that ship has

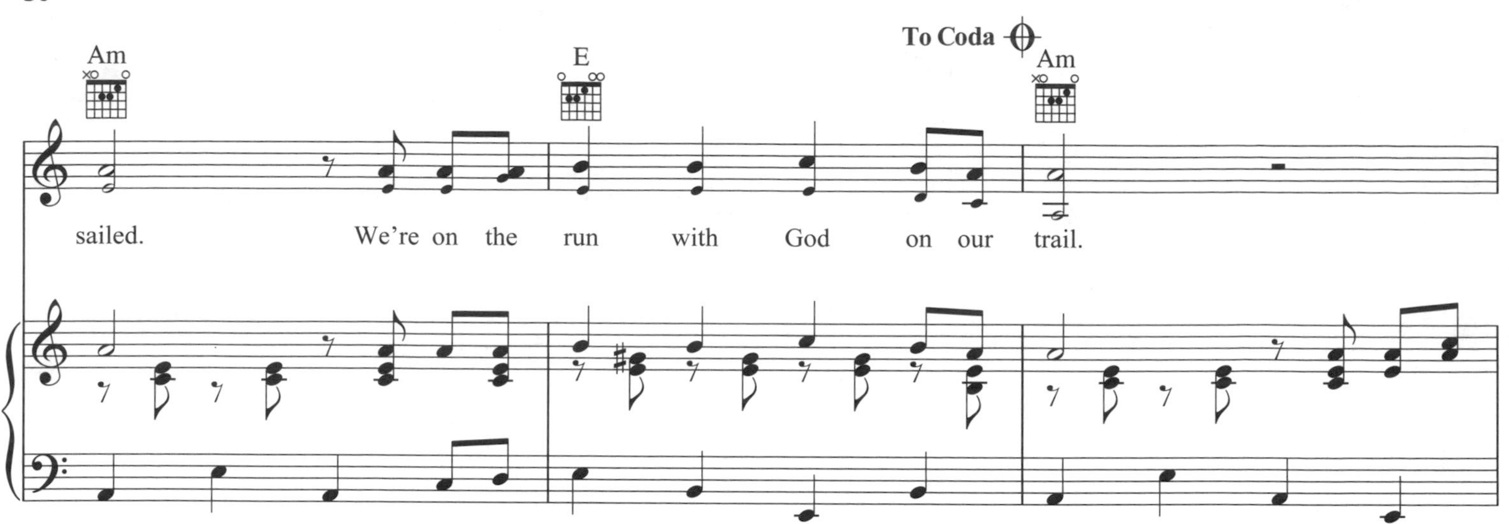
To Coda
Am
E
Am
sailed. We're on the run with God on our trail.

E

Am
Male:
Female:
Male:
I can re - mem - ber, I do re - call, there were no

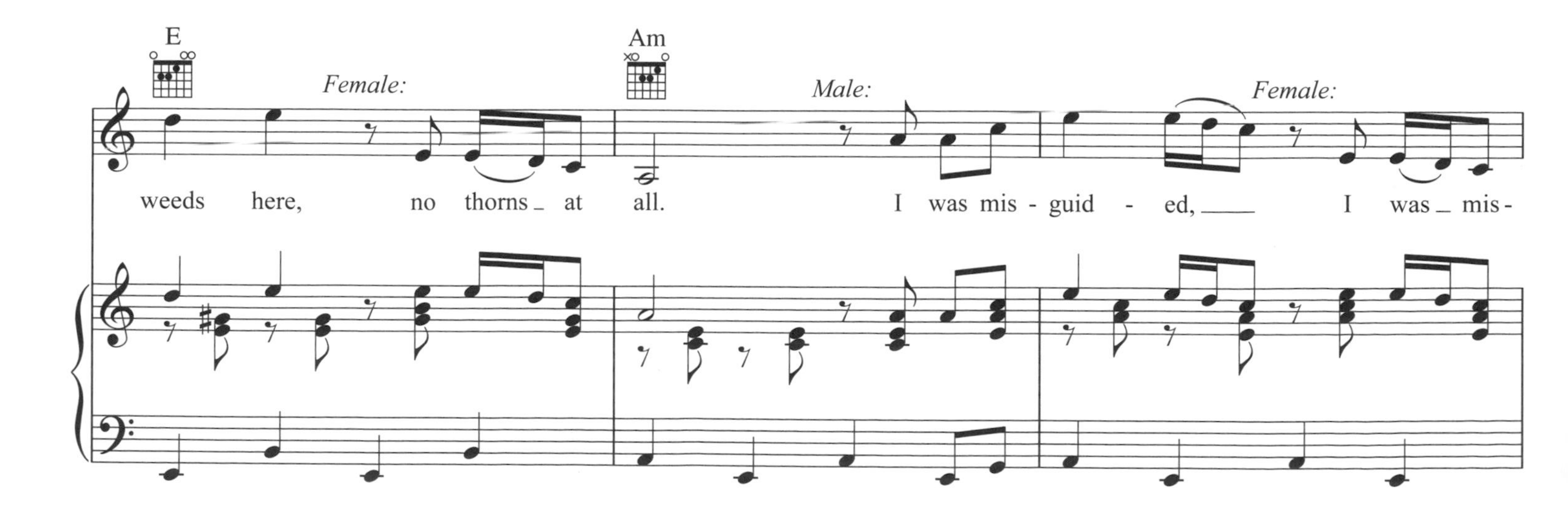
E
Am
Female:
Male:
Female:
weeds here, no thorns at all. I was mis - guid - ed, I was mis -

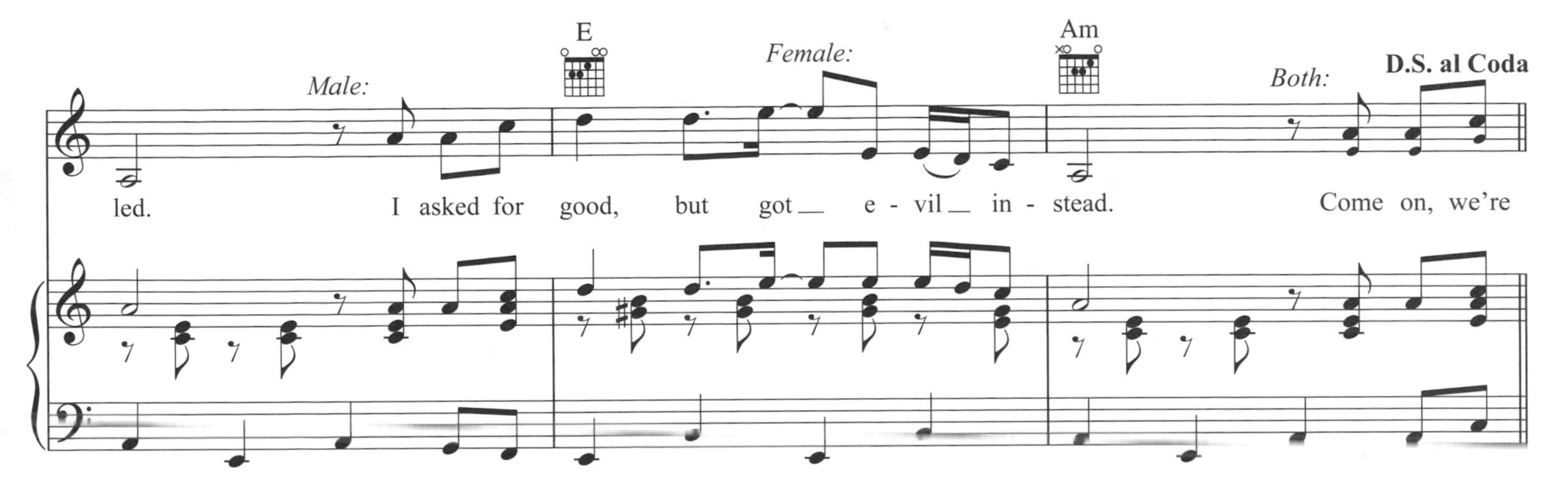
E
Am
Male:
Female:
Both:
D.S. al Coda
led. I asked for good, but got _ e - vil _ in - stead. Come on, we're

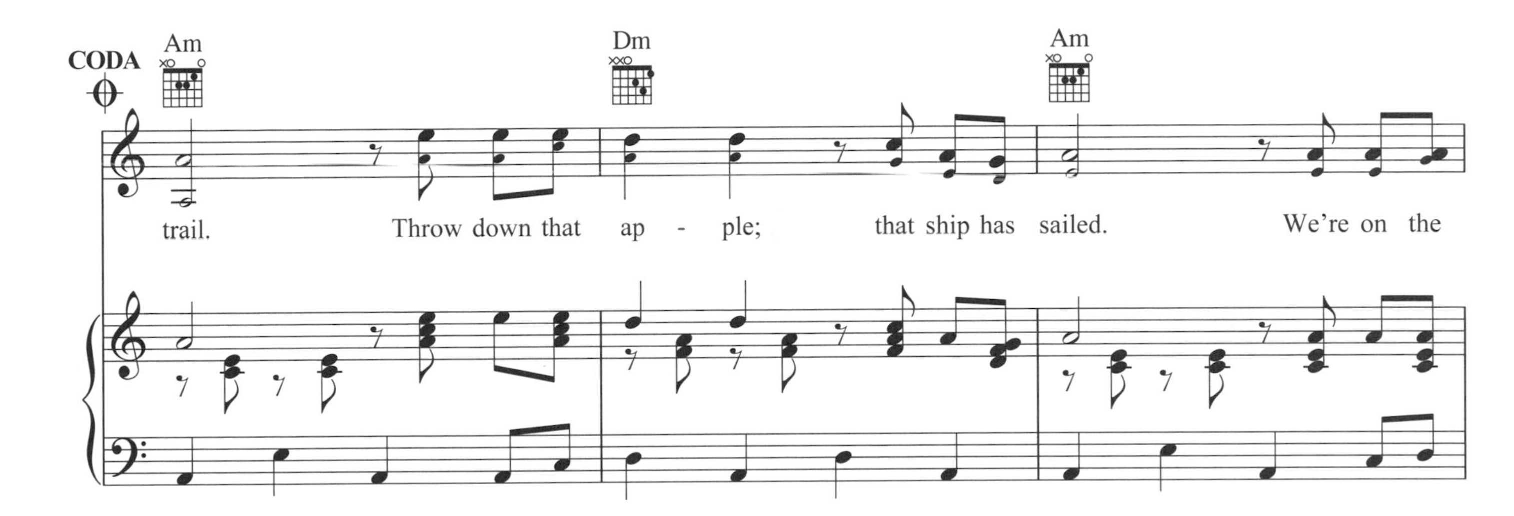
CODA
Am
Dm
Am
trail. Throw down that ap - ple; that ship has sailed. We're on the

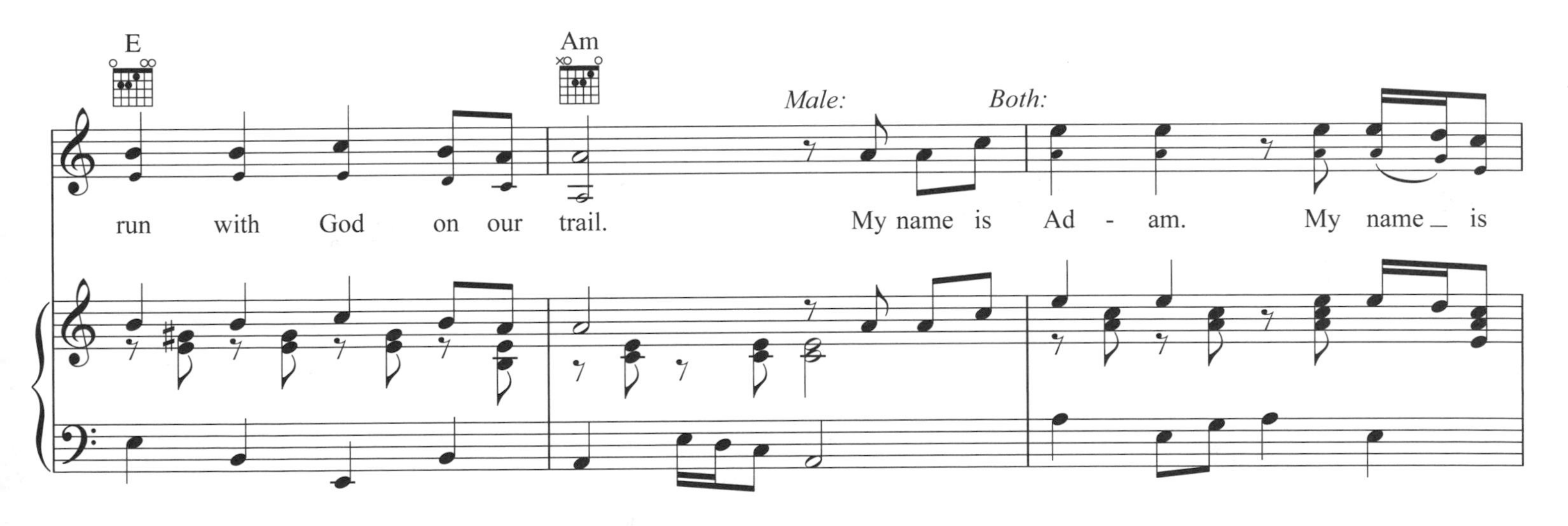
E
Am
Male:
Both:
run with God on our trail. My name is Ad - am. My name _ is

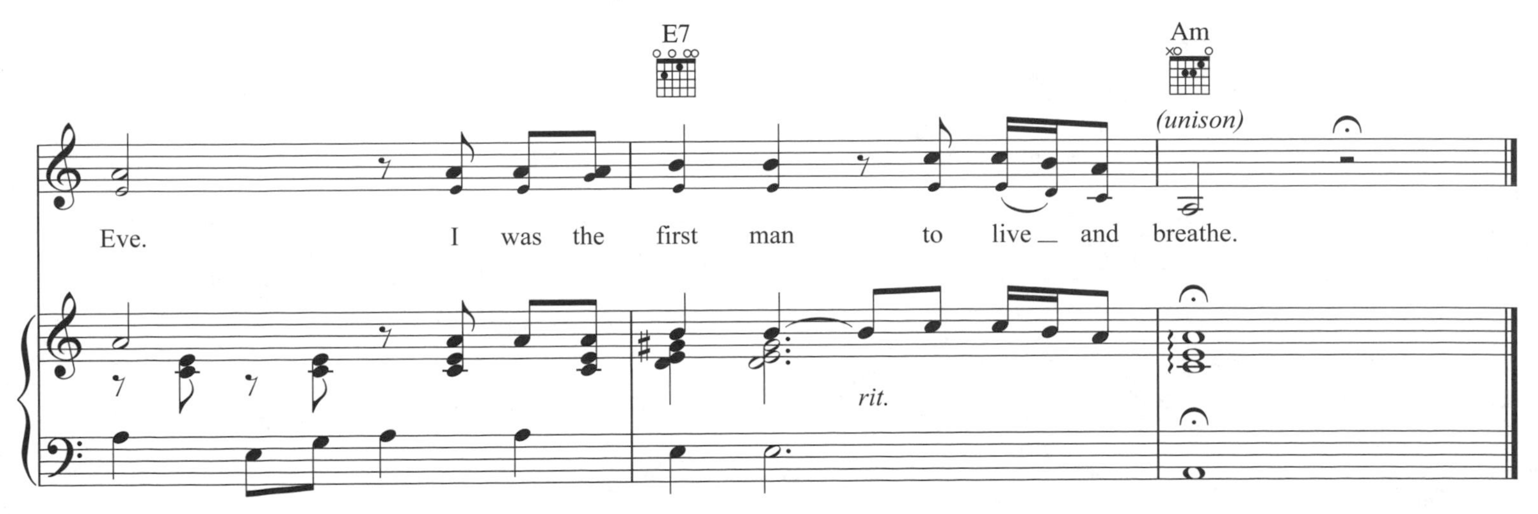
E7
Am
(unison)
Eve. I was the first man to live _ and breathe.
rit.

CALIFORNIA STARS

Words and Music by JAY BENNETT,
WOODY GUTHRIE and JEFFREY TWEEDY

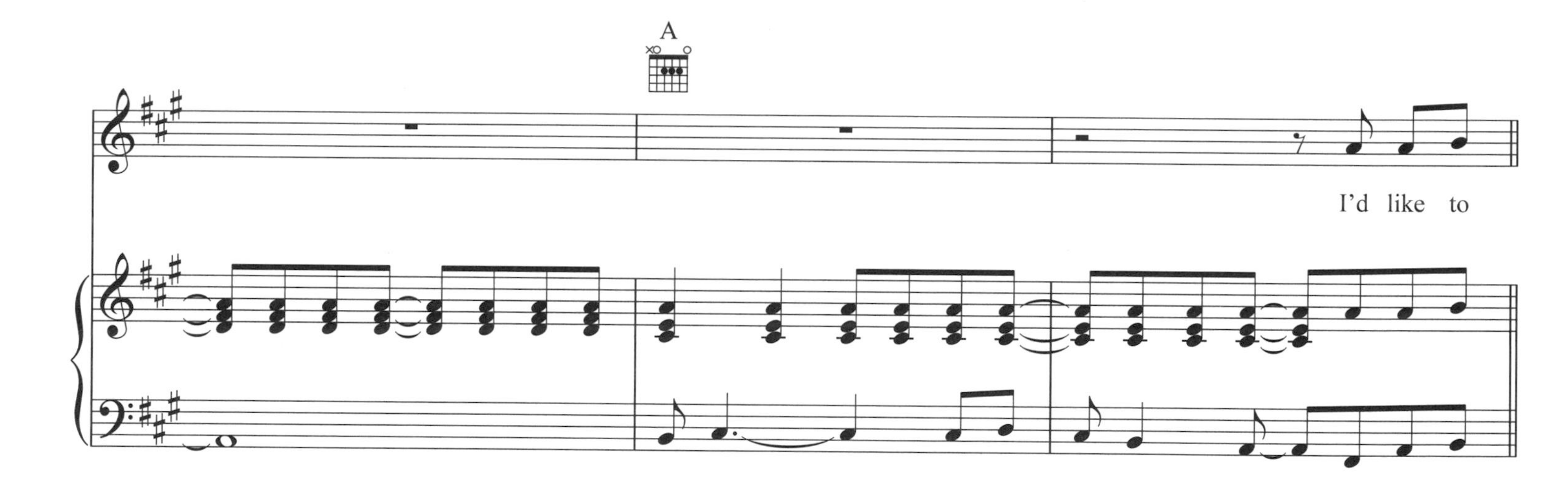

D
for - nia stars. I'd like to lay my wea - ry bones
for - nia stars and jump up from my star bed, make
A
to - night on a bed of Cal - i -
an - oth - er day un - der - neath my Cal - i -
for - nia stars. I'd love to feel your hand
for - nia stars. They hang like grapes on
E
touch - in' mine and tell me what I must keep
vines that shine and warm the lov - er's glass like

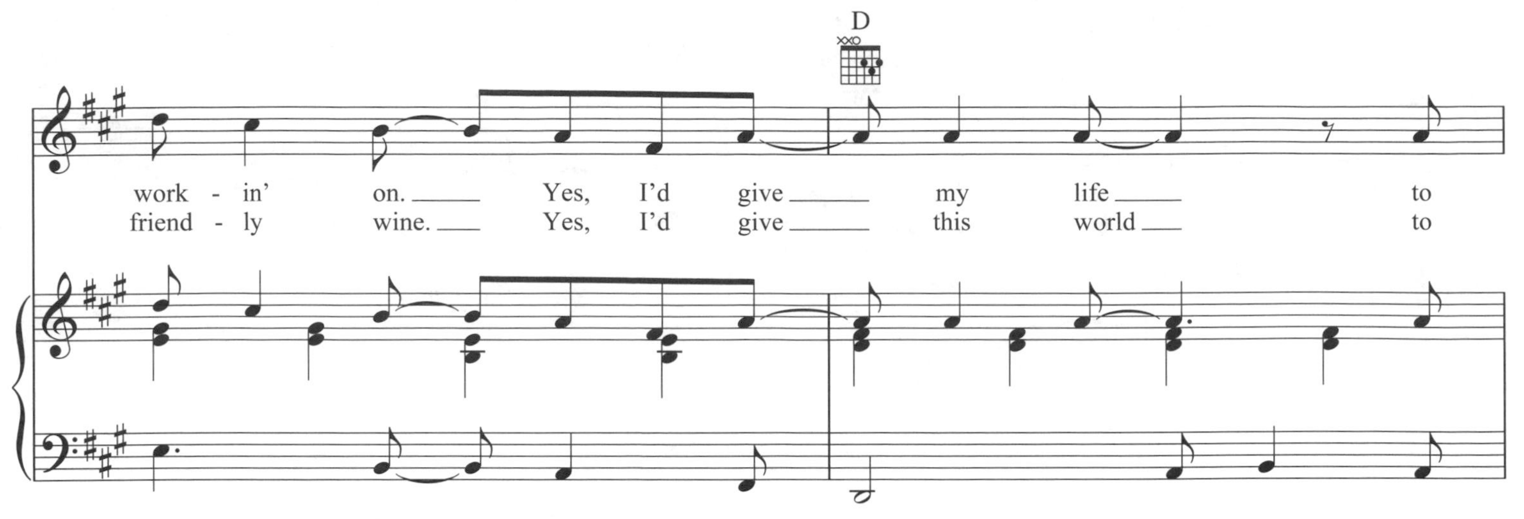
D
work - in' on. Yes, I'd give my life to
friend - ly wine. Yes, I'd give this world to

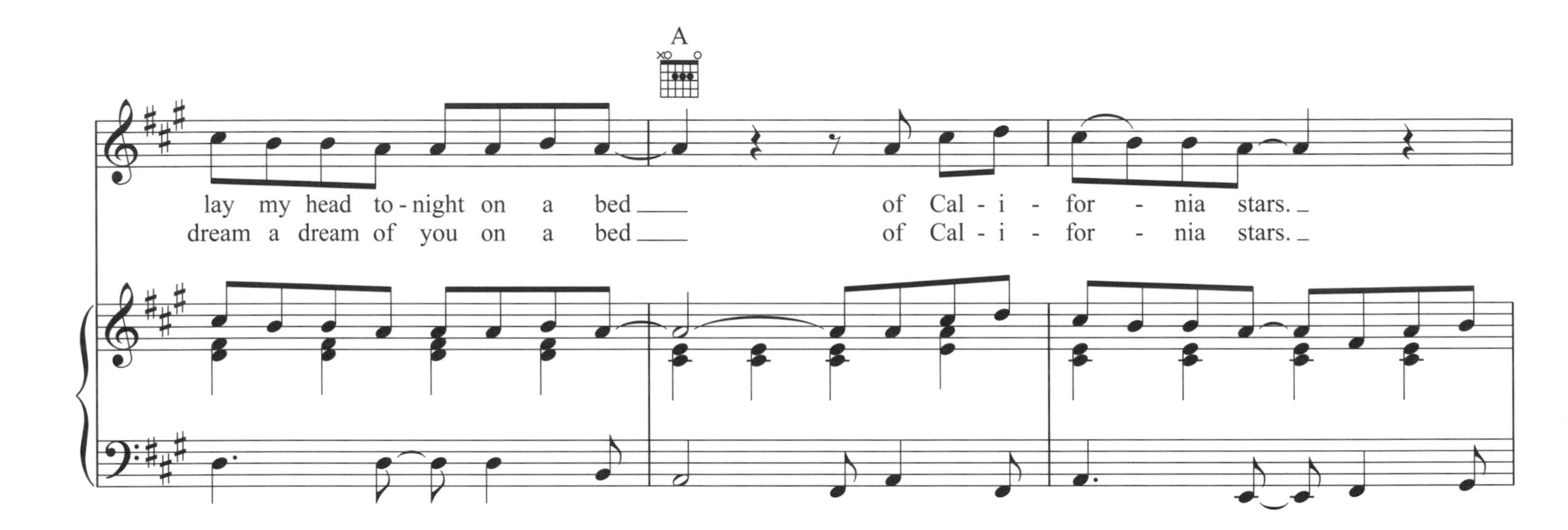
A
lay my head to-night on a bed of Cal - i - for - nia stars.
dream a dream of you on a bed of Cal - i - for - nia stars.

E

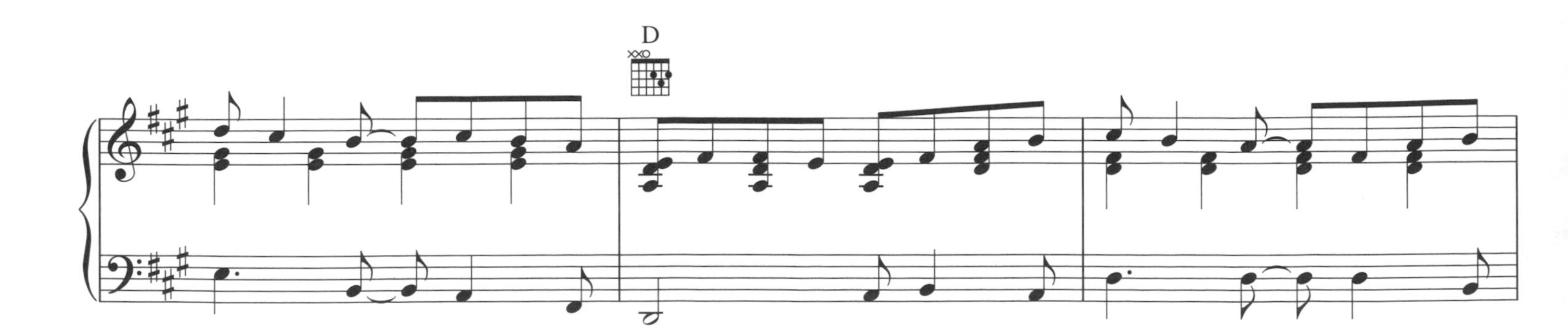
D

A
1–4
5
I'd like to

A
E

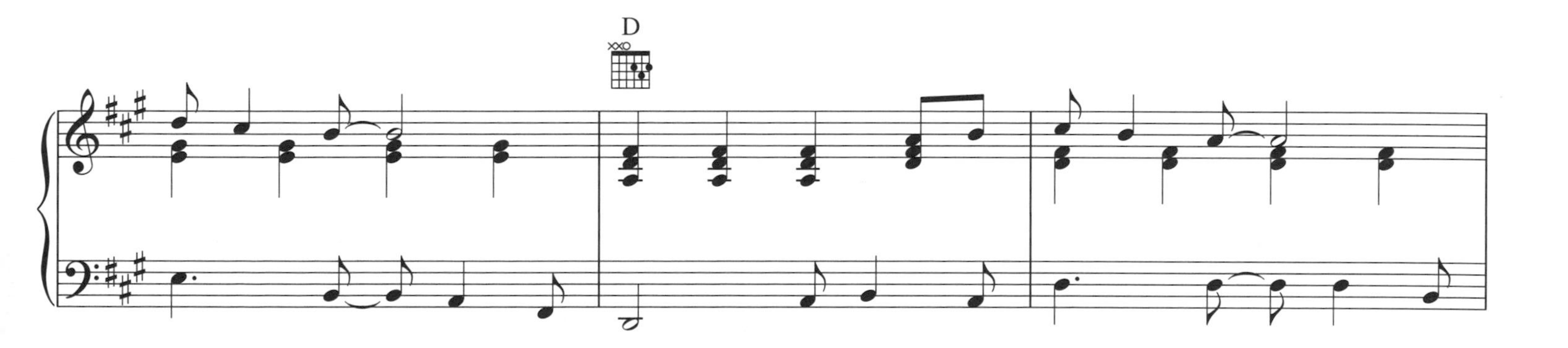
D

A
Repeat and Fade
Optional Ending

IT'S YOUR WORLD

Words and Music by
BOB SEGER

* Recorded a half step lower.

what we're gon - na eat.
Say a prayer for the vic - tims of ex - tinc - tion.
Say an - oth - er for the red - wood trees.
Say an - oth - er for the Arc - tic and the tun - dra.
Let's talk a - bout who we're tryin' to please. It's your world.
It's your world.
N.C.
B5
A5
5fr
B5

A5
5fr
It's your world. It's your

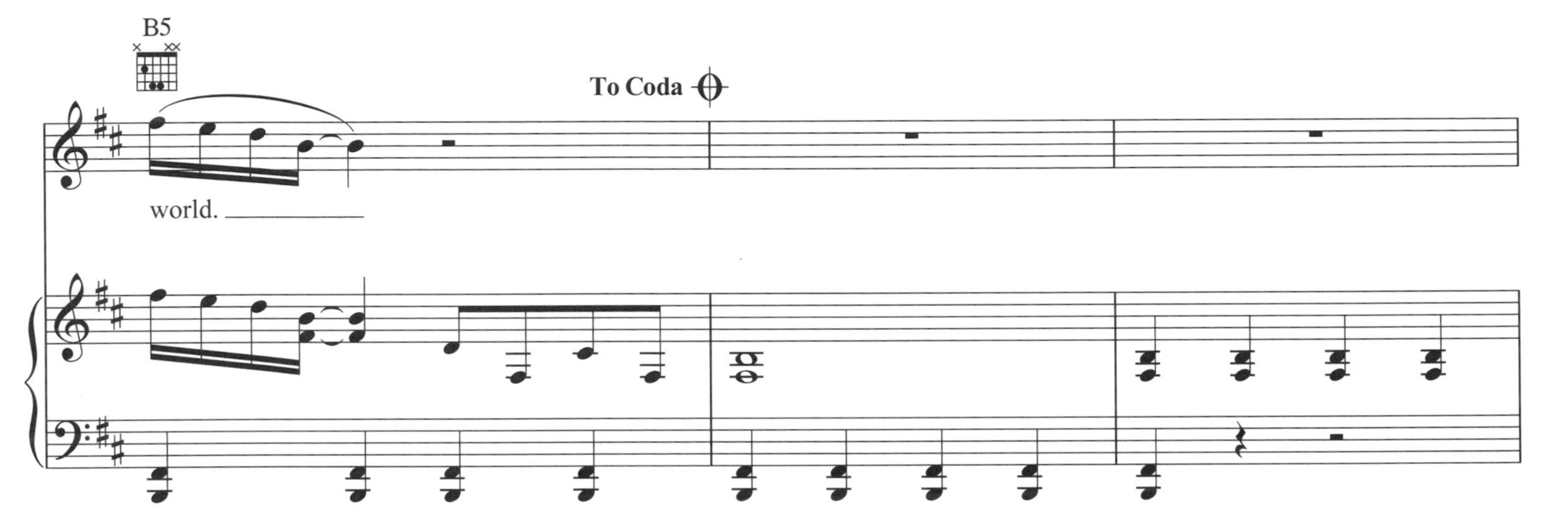
B5
To Coda
world.

The

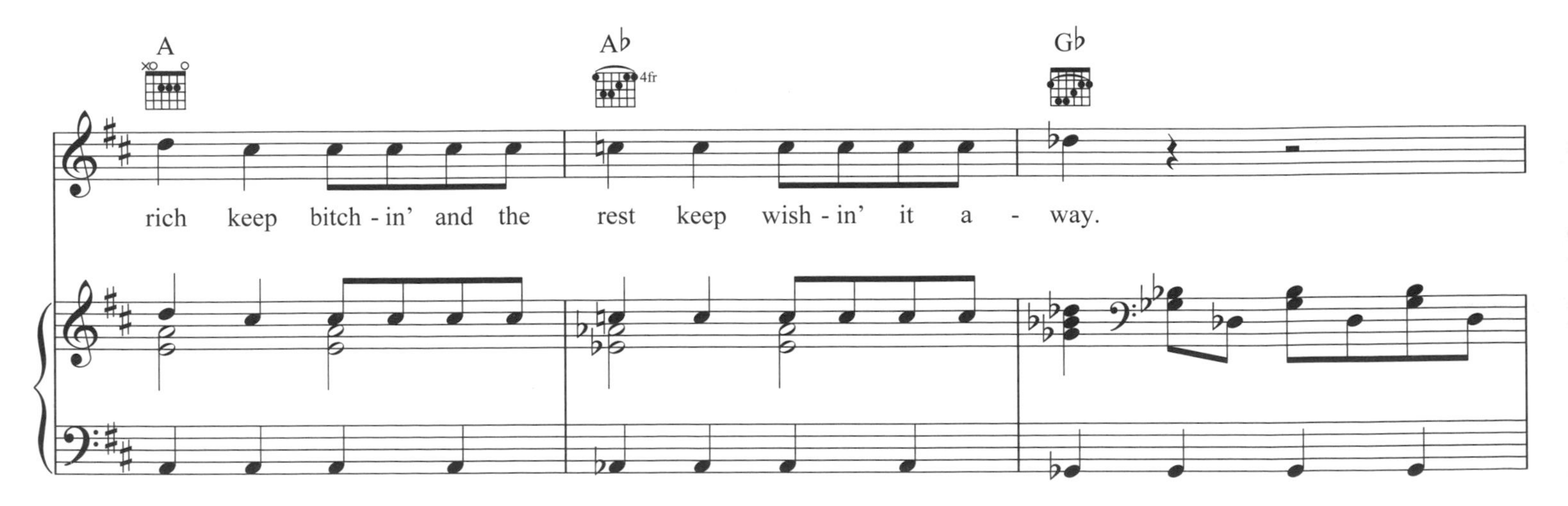
A
A♭
4fr
G♭
rich keep bitch - in' and the rest keep wish - in' it a - way.

A
E
All these chil - dren have to face our mess some -

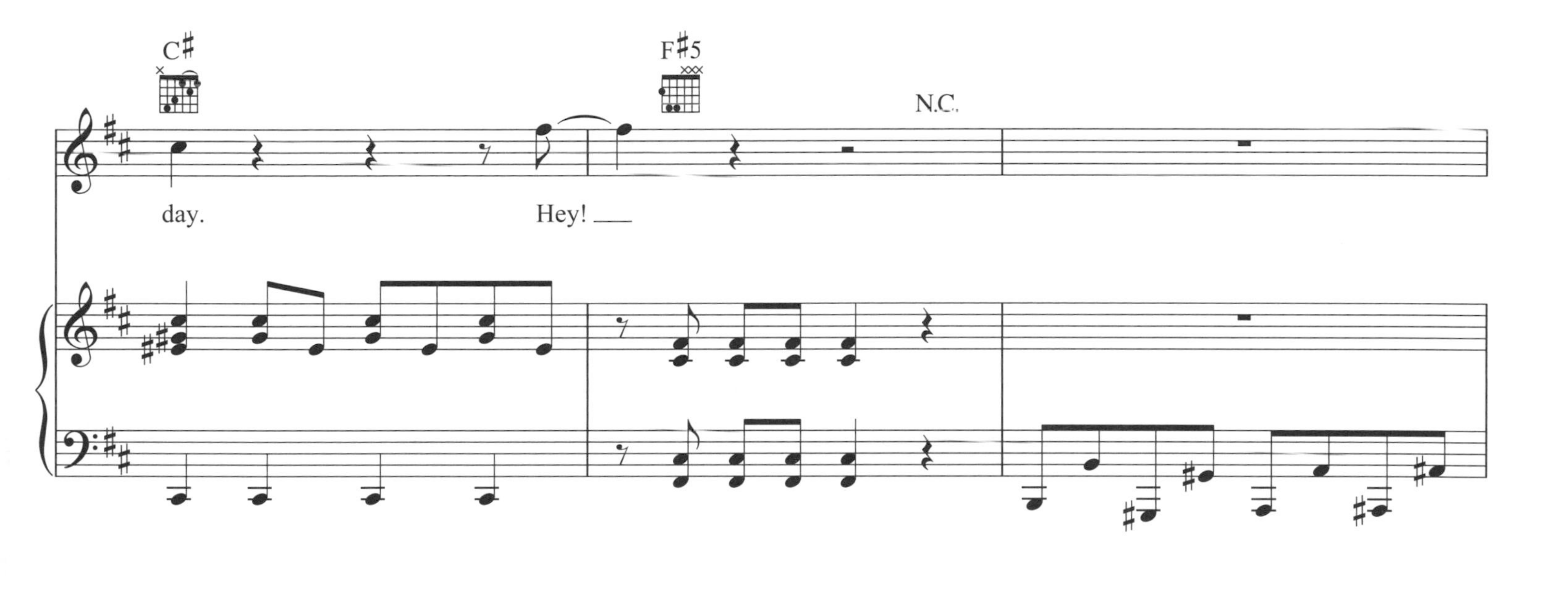
C♯
F♯5
N.C.
day. Hey!

B5
Let's talk a - bout min - ing in Wis - con - sin. Let's talk a - bout

breath - ing in Bei - jing.
Let's talk a - bout chem - i - cals in riv - ers.
Let's talk a - bout cash as king.
Let's talk a - bout

run - off from the moun - tains.
Check the lev - els on Lake Meade.

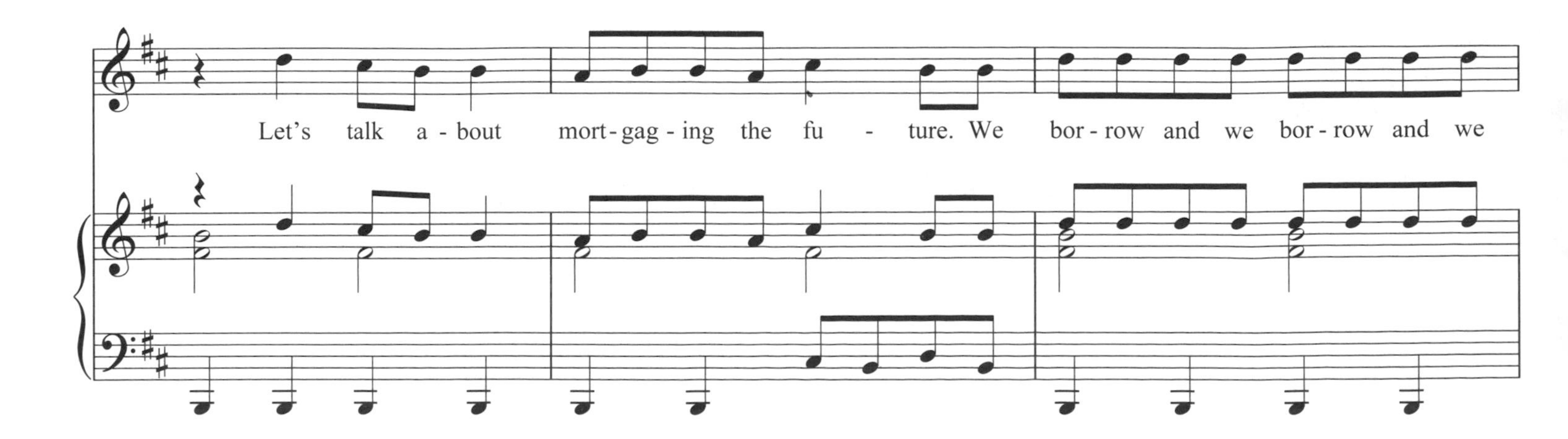
Let's talk a - bout mort - gag - ing the fu - ture. We bor - row and we bor - row and we

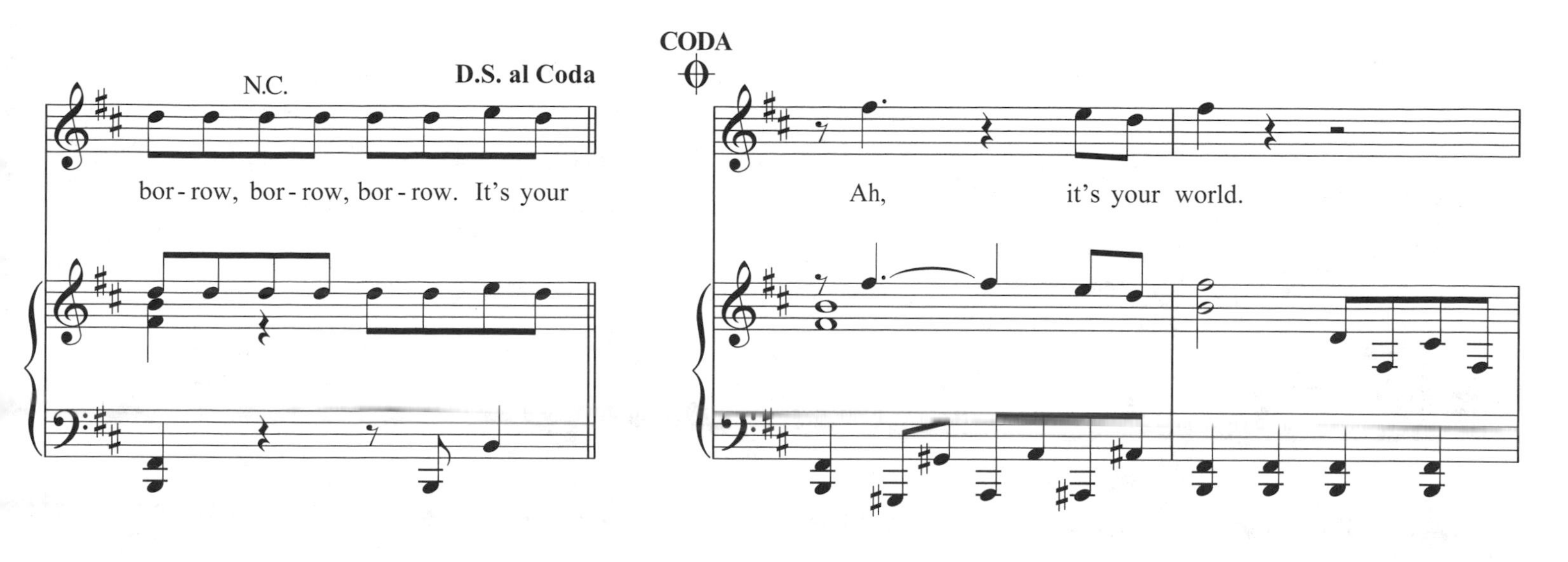
N.C.
D.S. al Coda
CODA
bor - row, bor - row, bor - row. It's your
Ah, it's your world.

A5
5fr
B5
It's your world.
It's your

A5
5fr
B5
world.
It's your world. _
Oh!

ALL OF THE ROADS

Words and Music by
BOB SEGER

* *Recorded a half step lower.*

G
C(add9)
hop-ing to leave my mark,
hop-ing I gave and I did-
may-be you'd un-der-stand;
ev-'ry mi-rage has a cer-
like from a dis-tant star,
cross-ing the void and ar-riv-
Em
D
C(add9)
-n't just take.
Climb-ing a moun-tain, man-
-tain ap-peal.
Af-ter the thrill, it's off
-ing one day.
O-ceans of space de-fend-
G
D
-y are left be-hind.
to in-dif-f'rent rooms.
-ing the great un-known.
8vb
Am
Em
F
To Coda
Chas-ing a dream and
see-ing the world takes
time.
Af-ter the lights, the
dark-ness is com-ing
soon.
Soon-er or lat-er,
all of us head for
home.

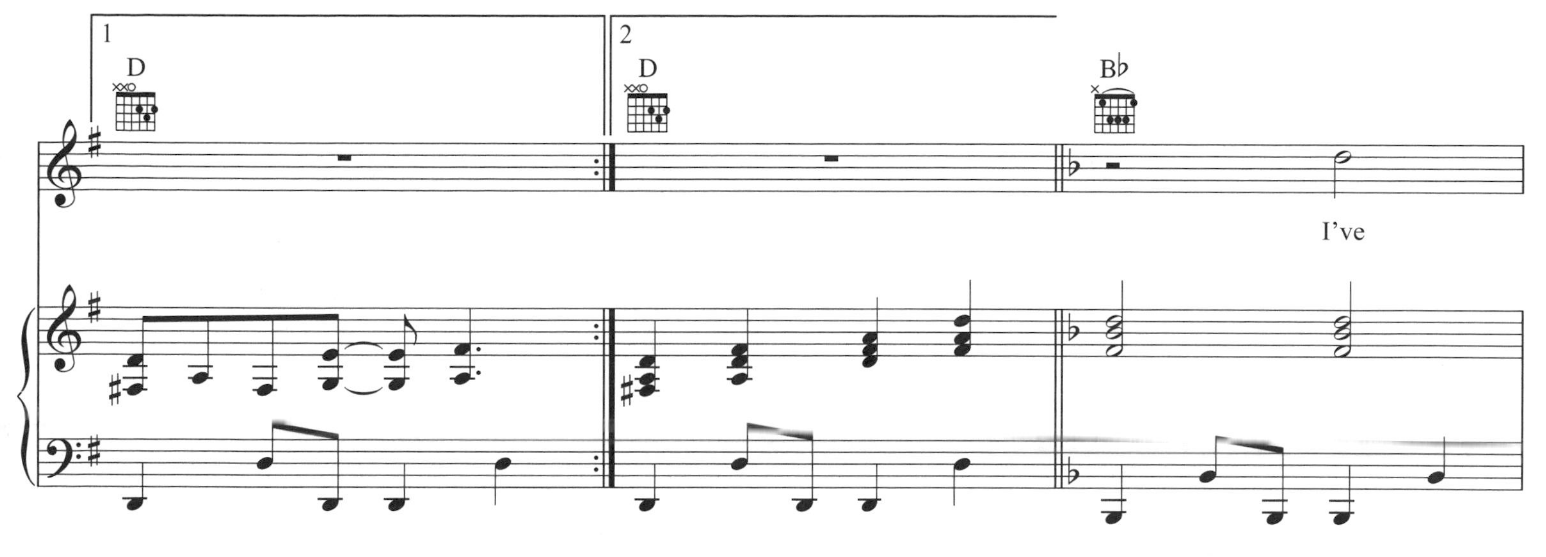
1
2
D
D
B♭
I've

C
F
Fsus2
F
done it all be - fore,

B♭
C
F
and I have gone to ev - 'ry door.

Fm
And I've been right down on the

C
G
floor
and more.
8vb

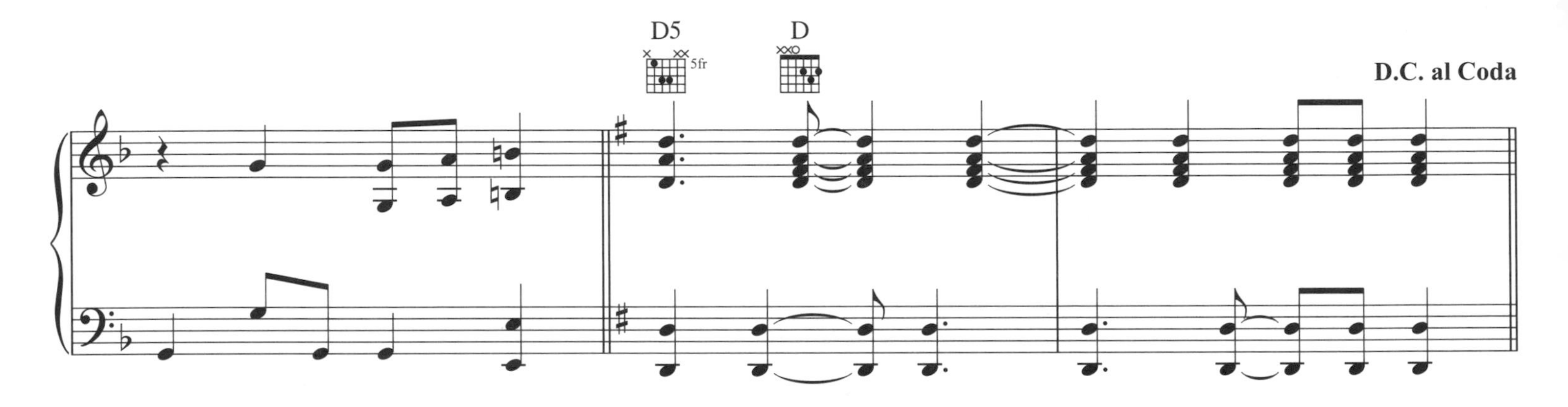
D5
5fr
D
D.C. al Coda

CODA
D
G
All of the roads I've run.

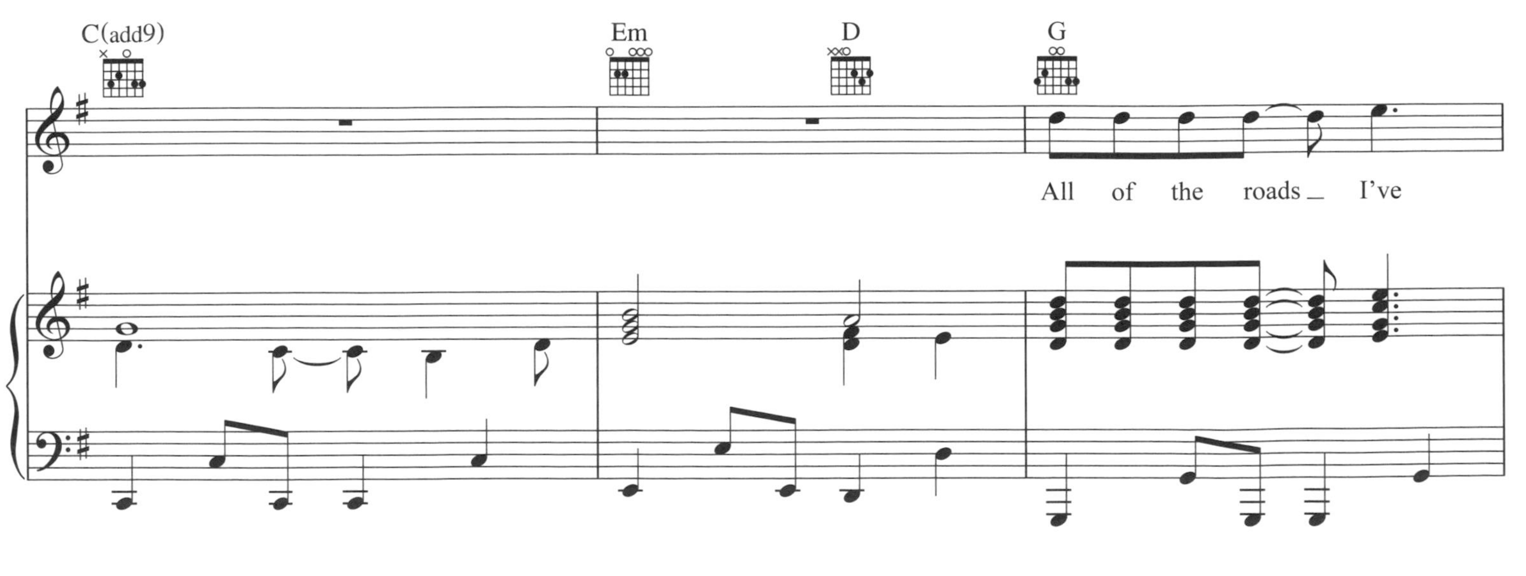
C(add9)
Em
D
G
All of the roads I've

C(add9)
Em
D
run.

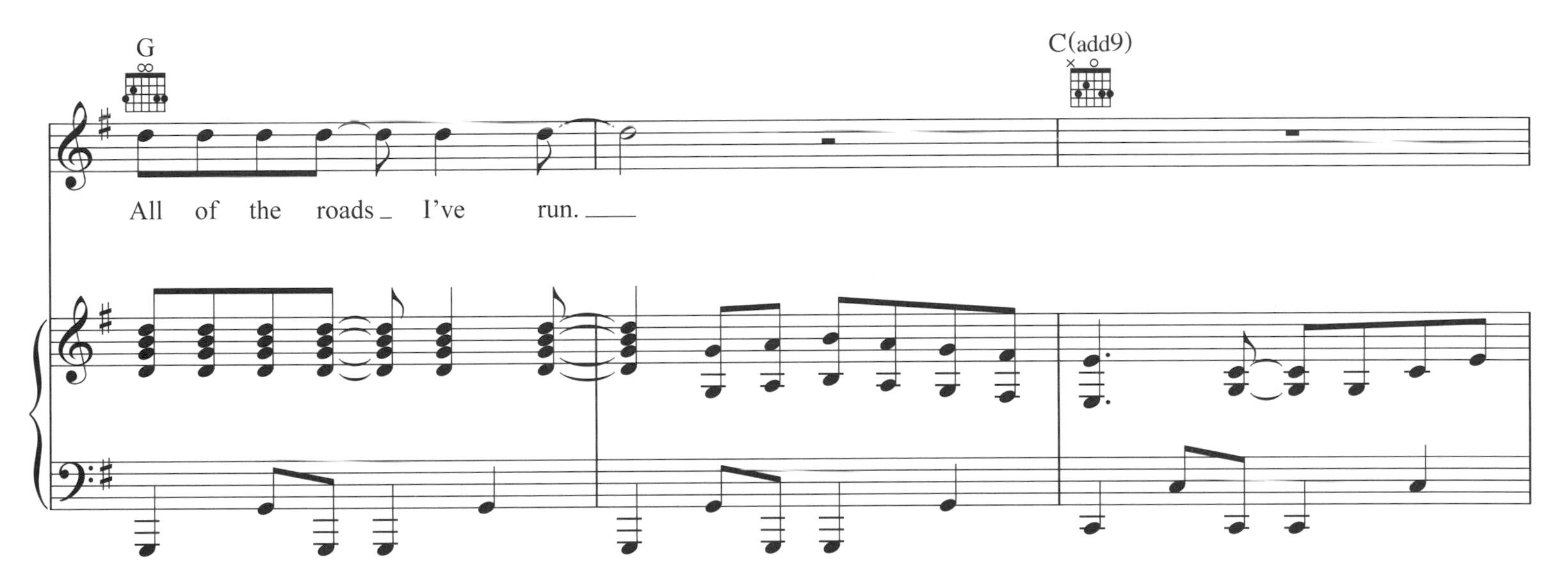
G
C(add9)
All of the roads _ I've run. ___

Em
D
G
All of the roads _ I've run.

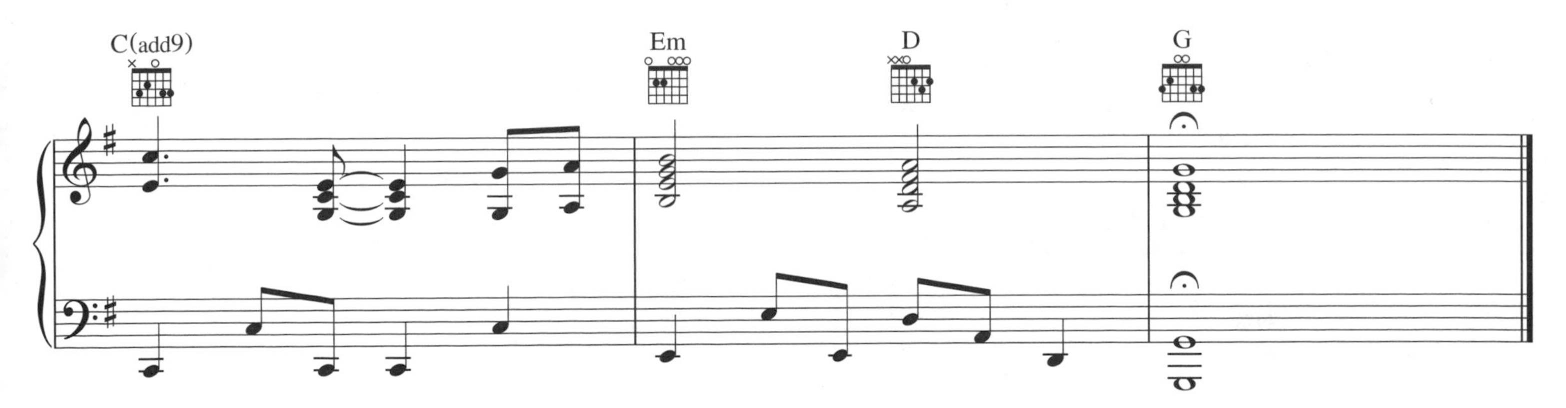
C(add9)
Em
D
G

YOU TAKE ME IN

Words and Music by
BOB SEGER

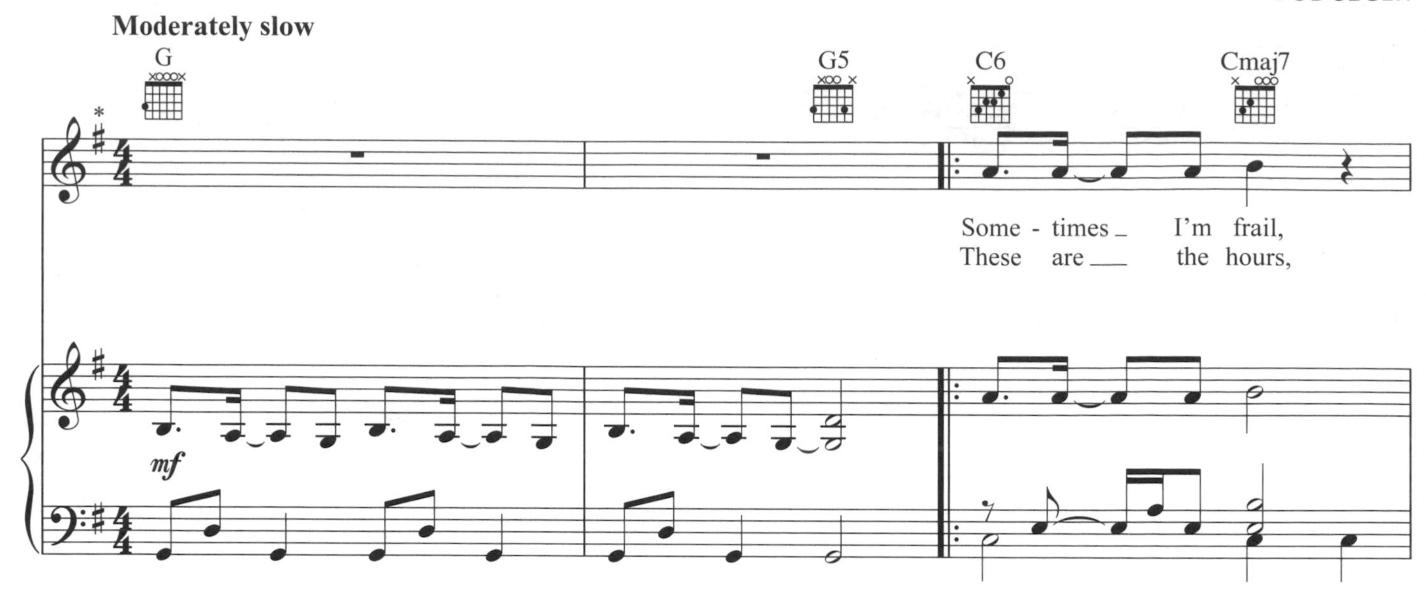

* *Recorded a half step lower.*

G/B
Am
high on a hill, making no dif - f'rence, im -
so much to feel, hav - ing a vi - sion and
G
G5
C(add9)
pos - ing no will. When prom - is - es scat - ter and
know - ing it's real. I search for the mean - ing and
G/B
Em
D/F♯
G
don't seem to mat - ter, I know, in the end,
keep on be - liev - ing be - cause, in the end,
Cmaj7
G
C(add9)
you take me in. Through all of this van - i - ty,
you take me in. Through all of these rea - sons that

G/B
Em
D/F♯
G
all this in - san - i - ty, I've got a friend.
change like the sea - sons, I've got a friend.
Cmaj7
G5
Cmaj7
G
You take me in.
You take me in. You take me in.
Cmaj7
You take me in.

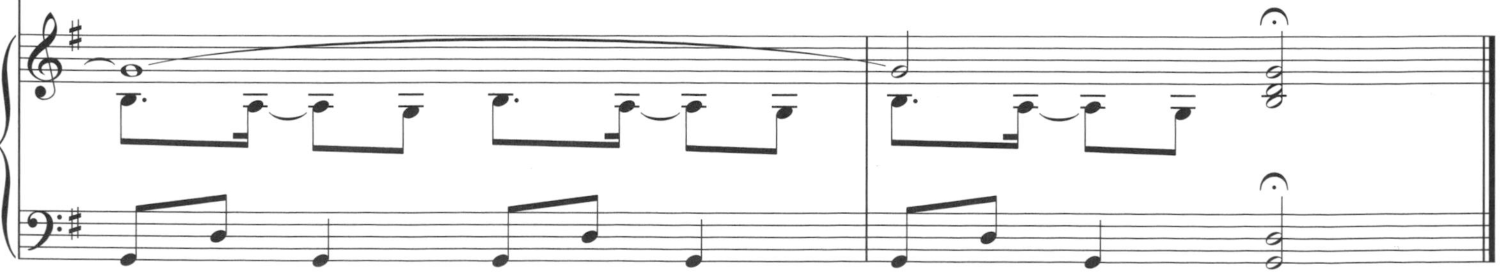
G

GATES OF EDEN

Words and Music by
BOB SEGER

* Recorded a half step lower.

G5
I re - mem - ber think - ing all of this must have a rea -
I re - mem - ber search - ing, long - ing for a deep - er mean -
(8vb)
D5
G5
D5
- son.
- ing,
and it
I re - mem - ber think - ing may -
hit me like a dia - mond bul -
A5
1
D5
- be I should look be - yond.
- let right be - tween the eyes.
But
2
D5
D
And I be - lieve

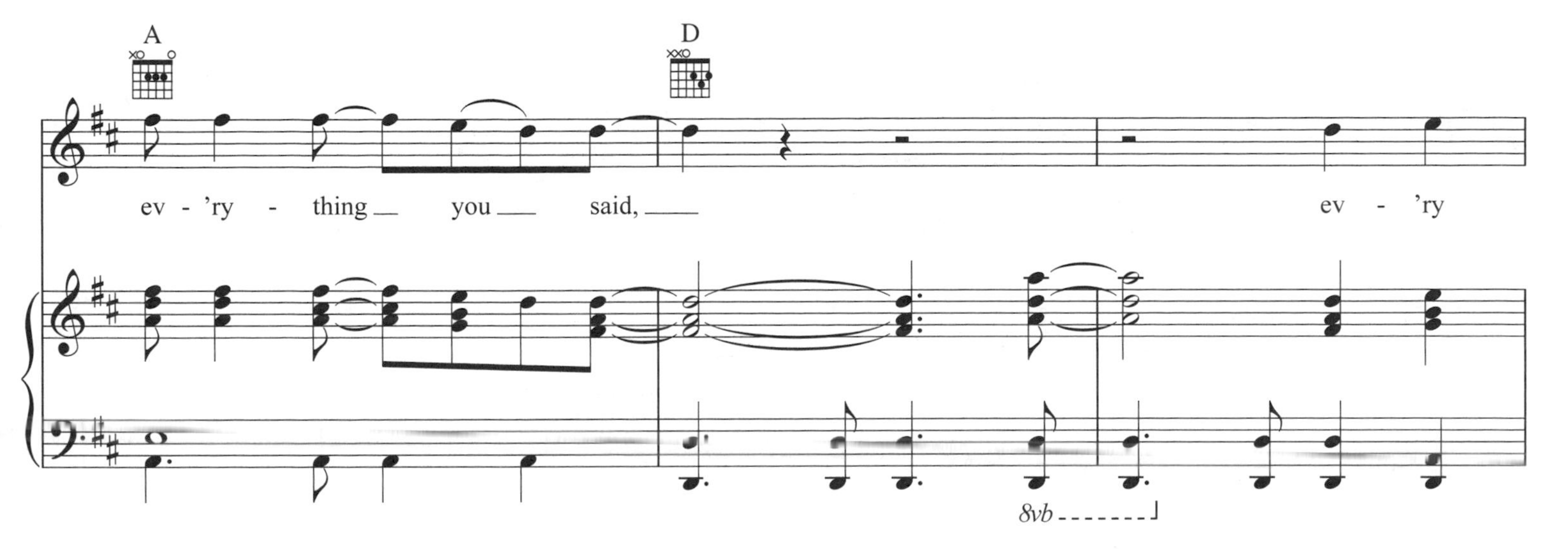
A
D
ev - 'ry - thing __ you __ said, __
ev - 'ry
8vb

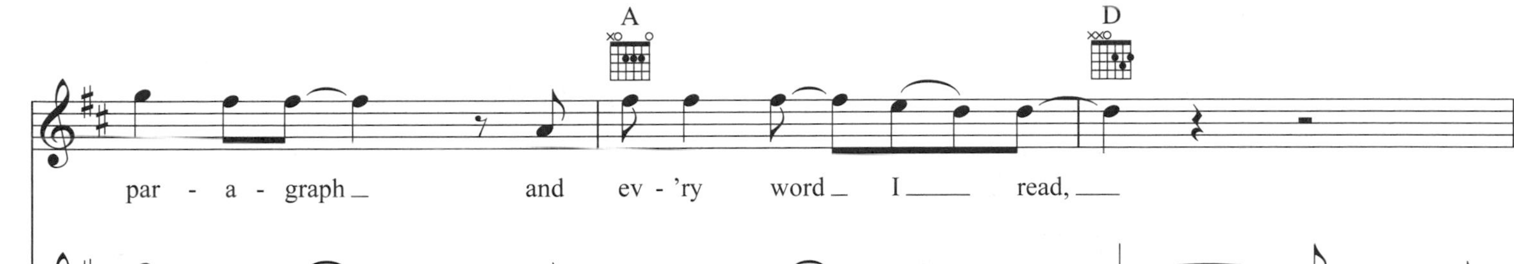
A
D
par - a - graph __ and ev - 'ry word __ I __ read, __

8vb

G
call - ing in - to ques - tion ev - 'ry - thing that I be - lieved __

(8vb)

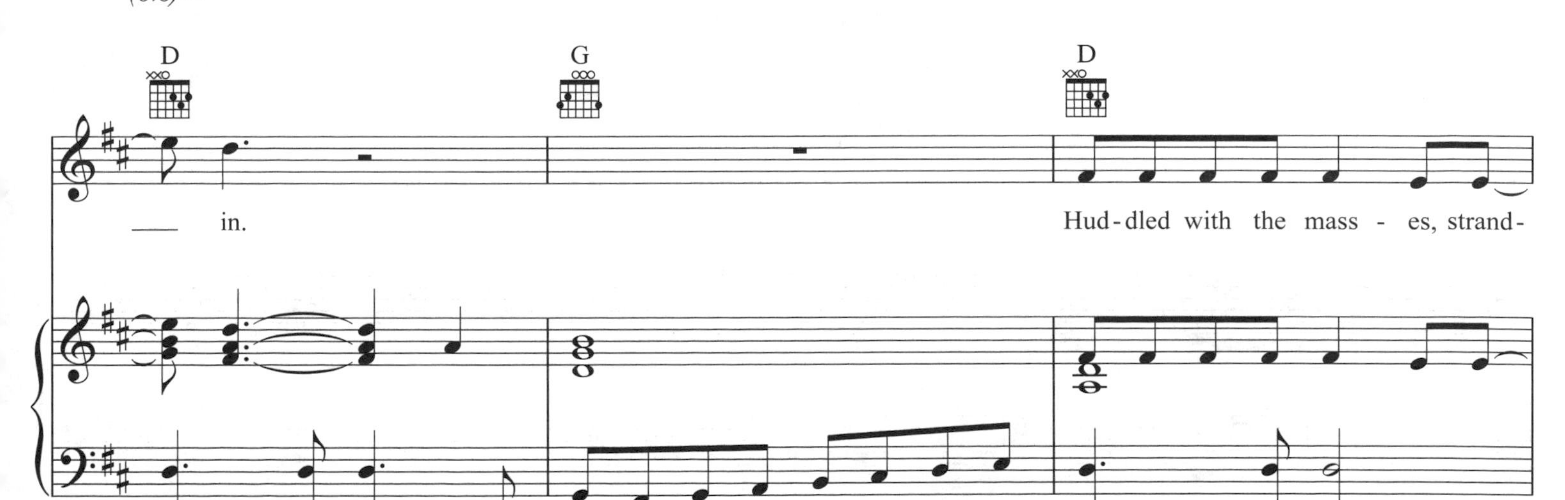
D
G
D
__ in.
Hud - dled with the mass - es, strand -

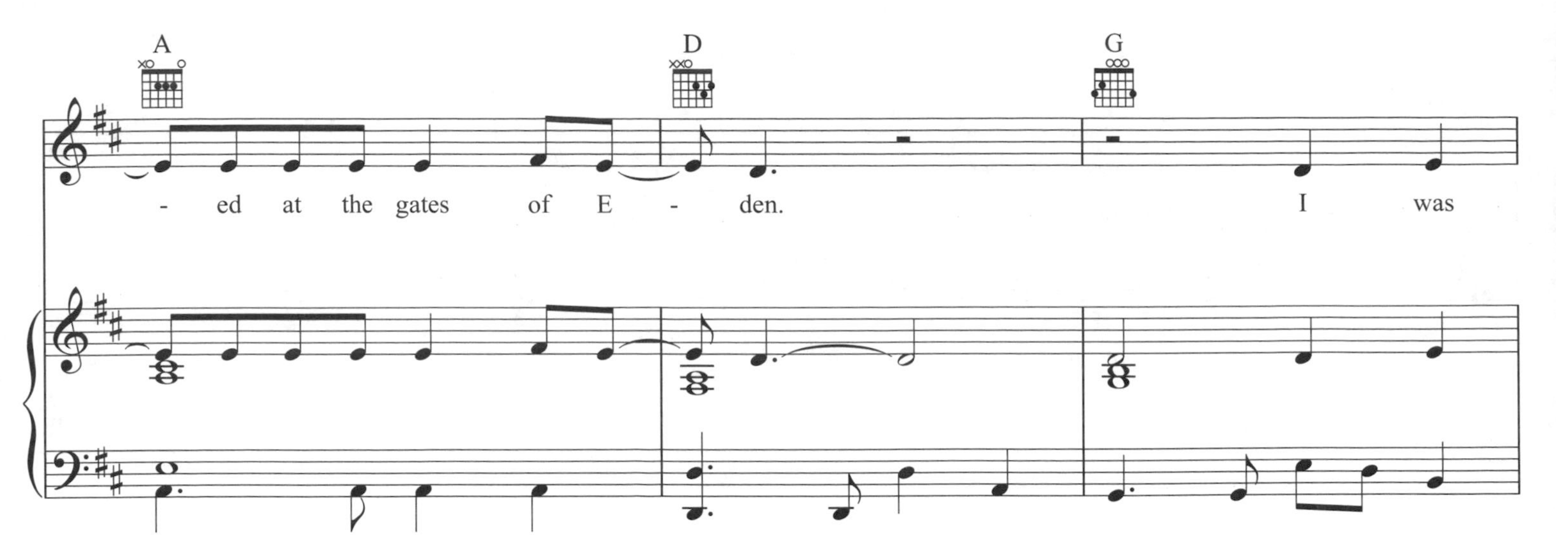
A
D
G
- ed at the gates of E - den. I was

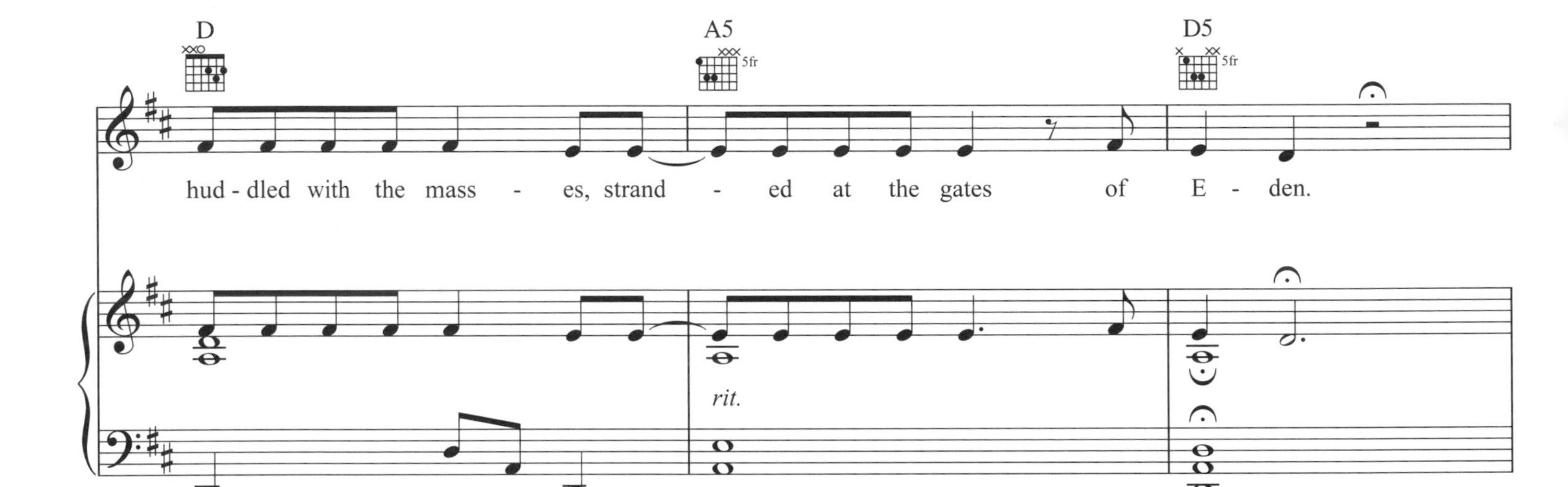
D
A5
5fr
D5
5fr
hud - dled with the mass - es, strand - ed at the gates of E - den.
rit.

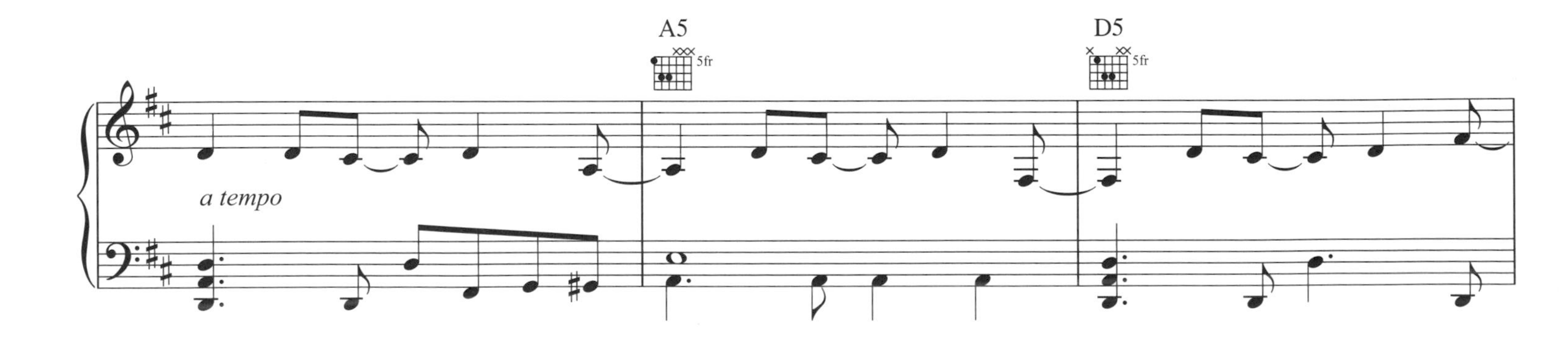
A5
5fr
D5
5fr
a tempo

A5
5fr

D5
5fr
G

D
G

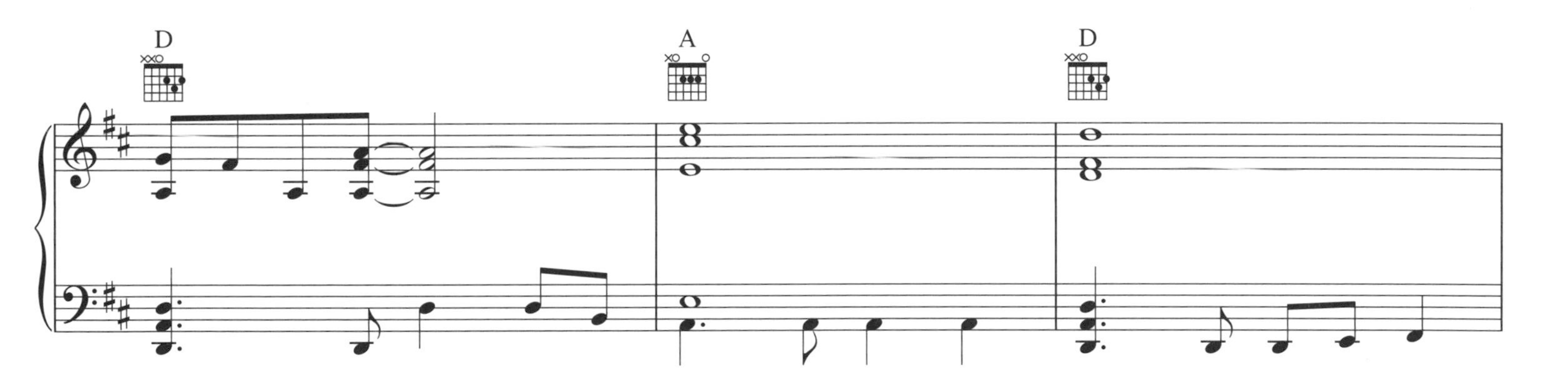
D
A
D

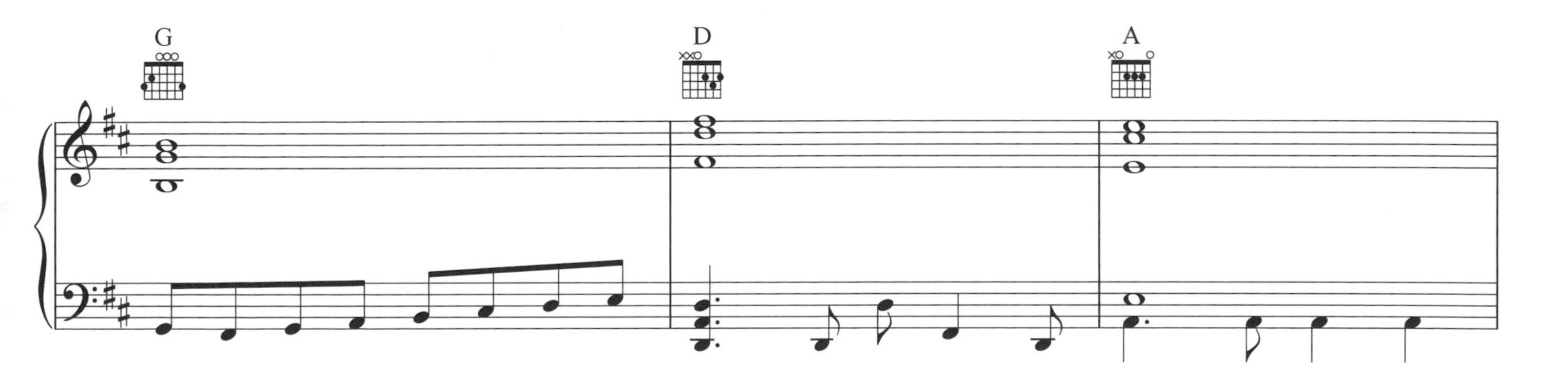
G
D
A

D5
5fr

LISTEN

Words and Music by
BOB SEGER

C6
B♭6
F
real - ly take the time,
dark - ness dies at dawn,
words be - come un - clear,

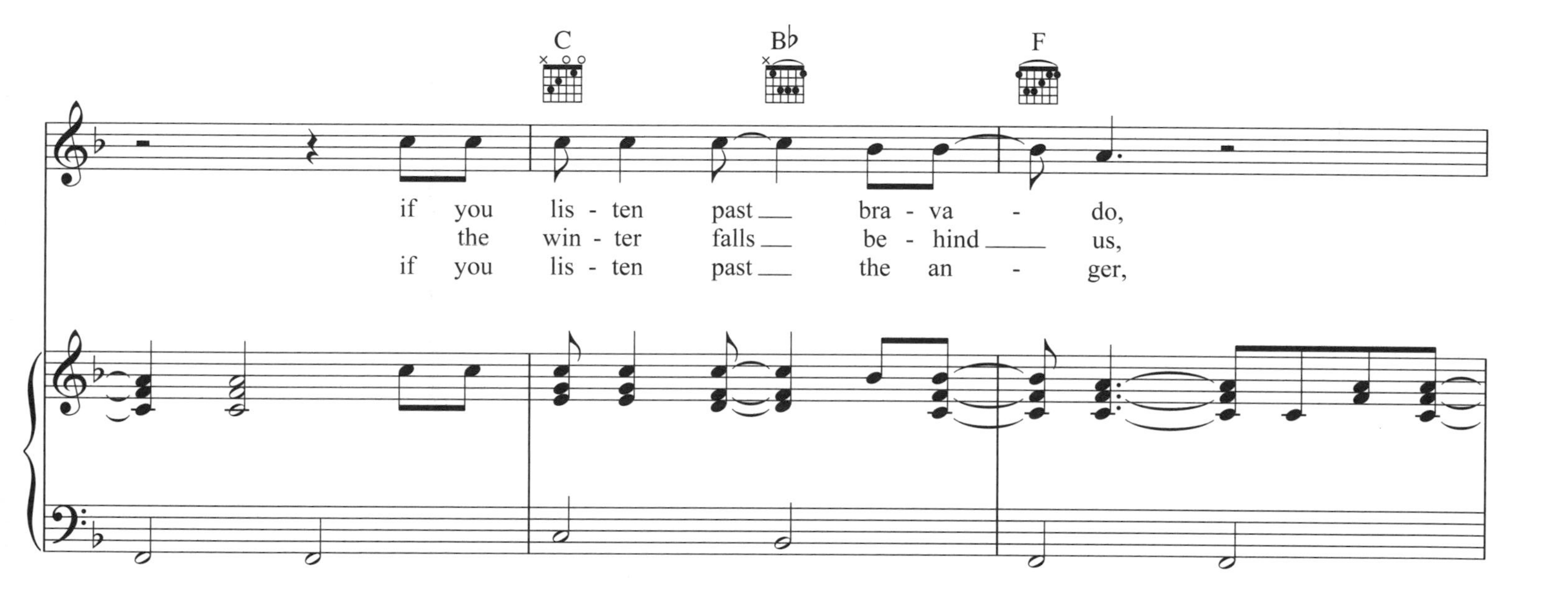

C
B♭
F
if you lis - ten past bra - va - do,
the win - ter falls be - hind us,
if you lis - ten past the an - ger,

C6
B♭6
if you lis - ten past the wine.
and the sum - mer comes a - long.
if you lis - ten past the fear,

F
Dm
F
Ev - 'ry - one's so bus - y,
We all need be - liev - ing,
ev - 'ry - one's e - lus - ive,
B♭
C
the truth gets left be - hind,
so we can car - ry on,
but the truth is al - ways near.
If you
F
left be - hind.
car - ry on.
lis - ten, you will hear.

1
2, 3

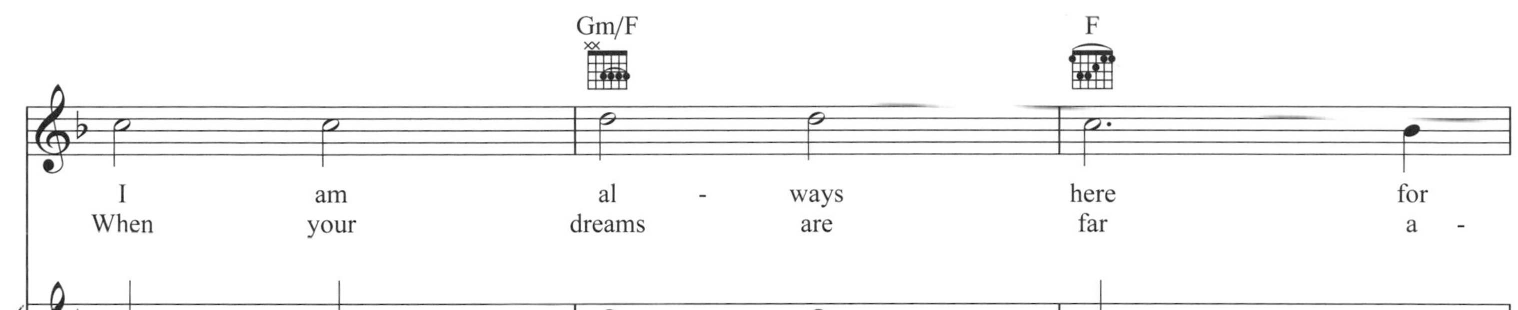
Gm/F
F
I am al - ways here for
When your dreams are far a -

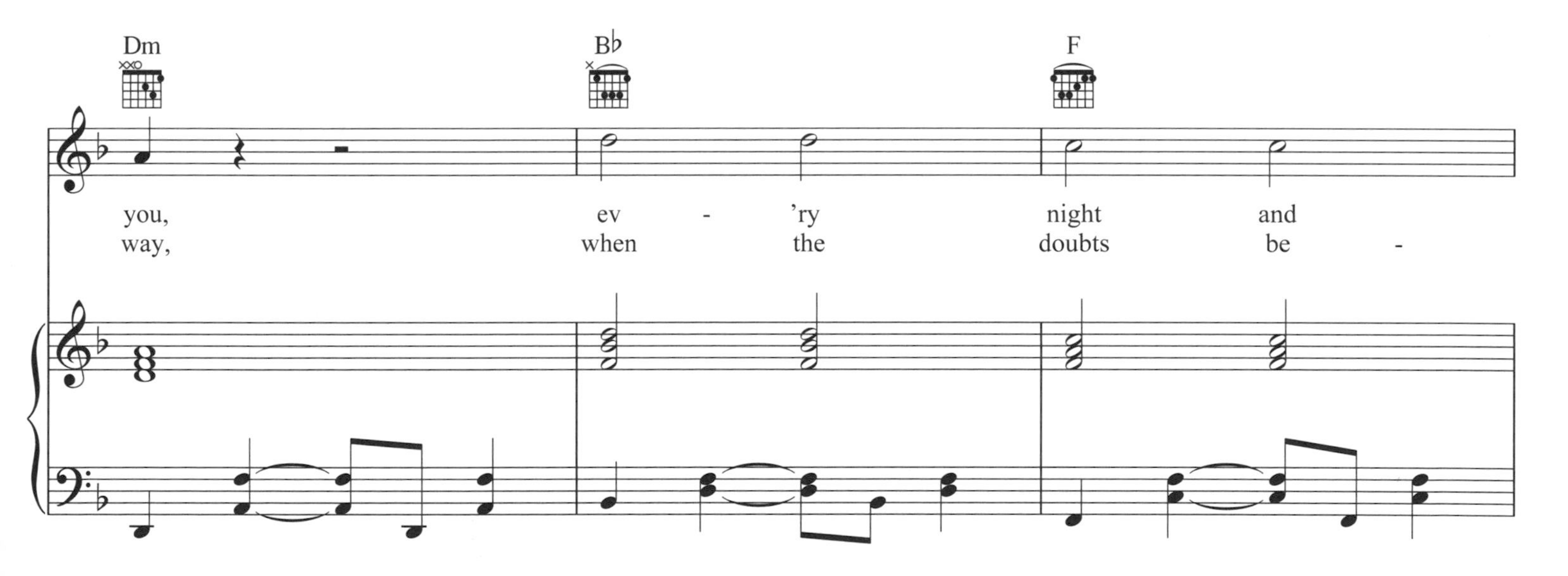
Dm
B♭
F
you, ev - 'ry night and
way, when the doubts be -

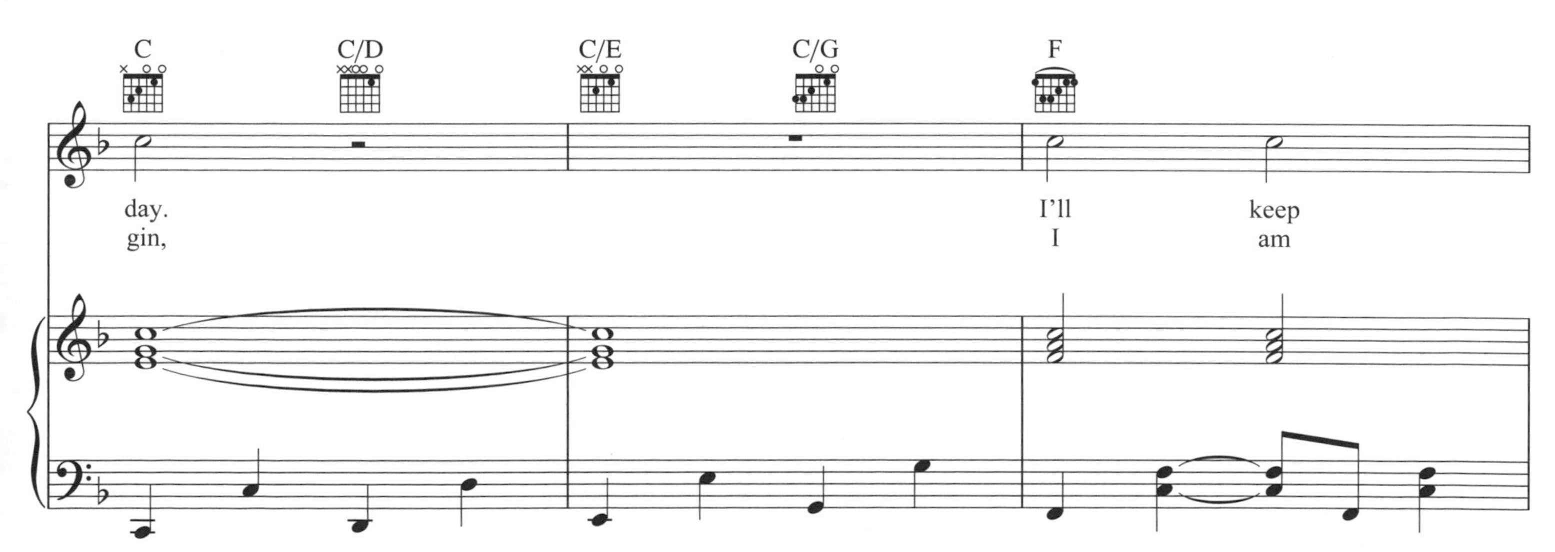
C
C/D
C/E
C/G
F
day. I'll keep
gin, I am

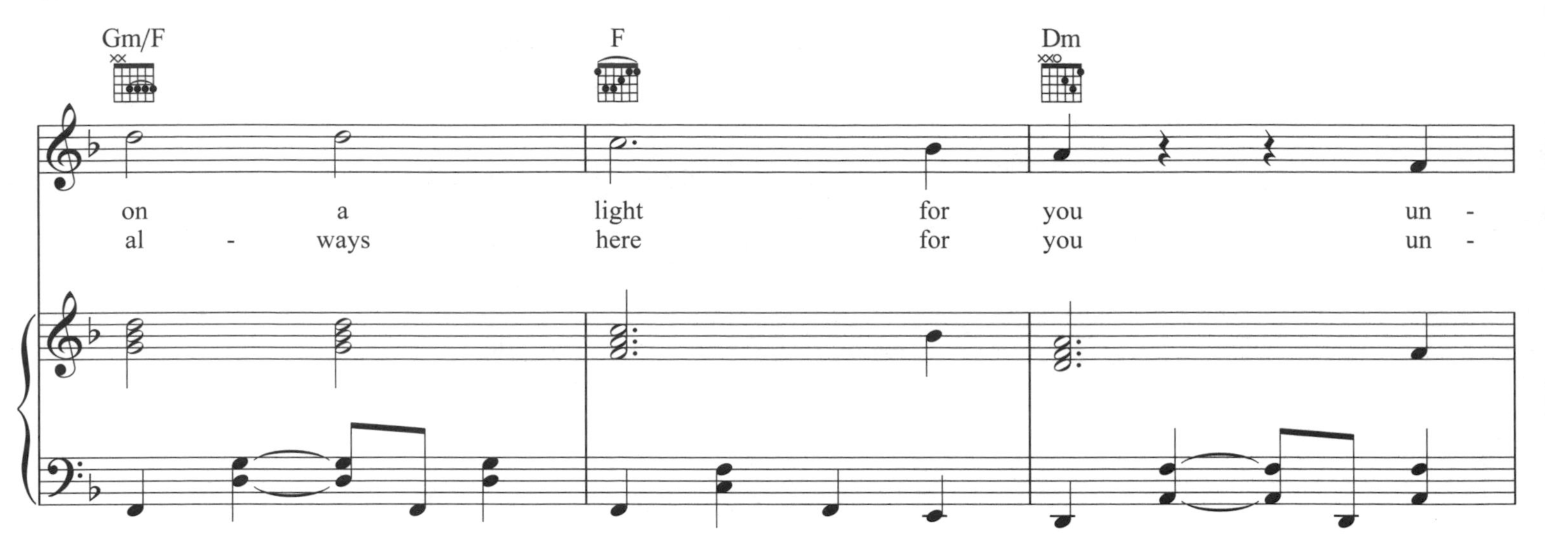
Gm/F
F
Dm
on a light for you un -
al - ways here for you un -

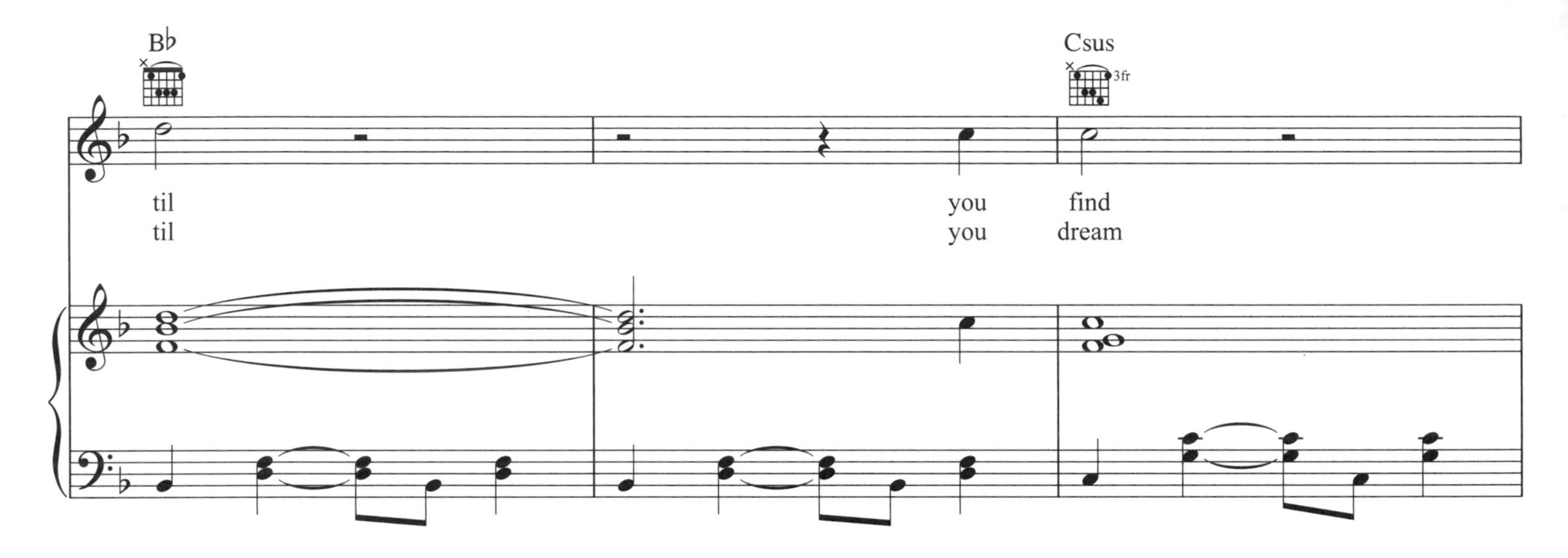
B♭
Csus
3fr
til you find
til you dream

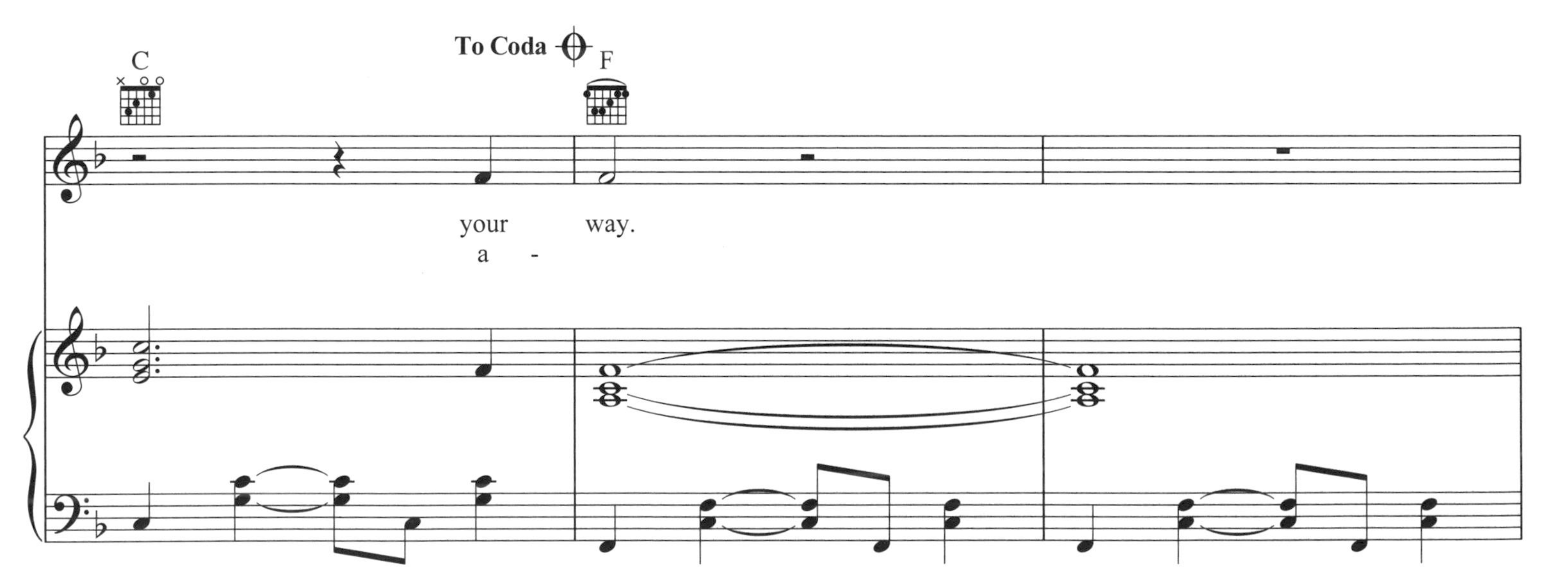
C
To Coda
F
your way.
a -

C
B♭

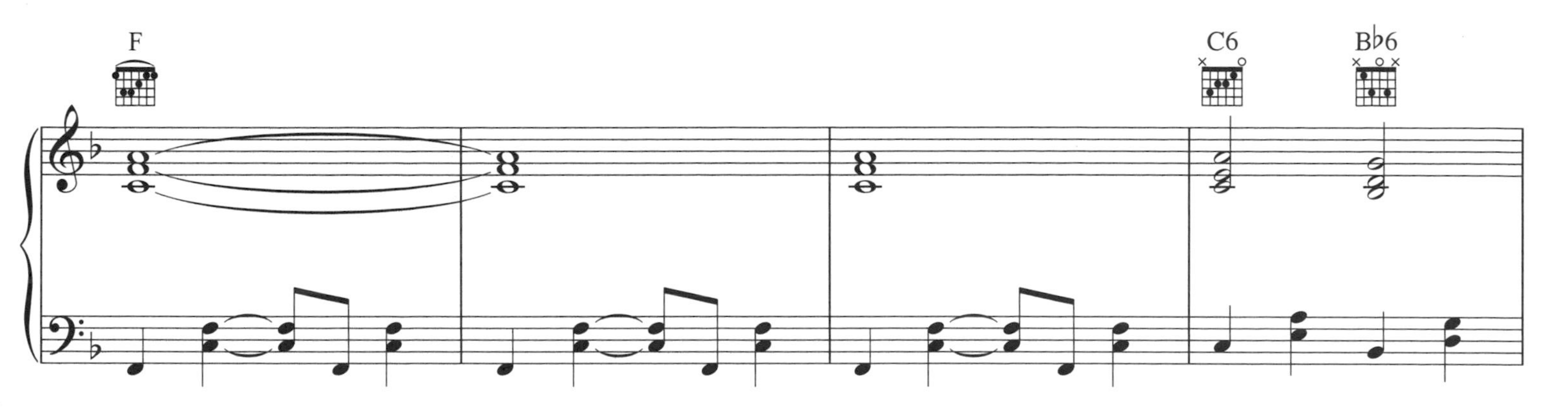
F
C6
B♭6

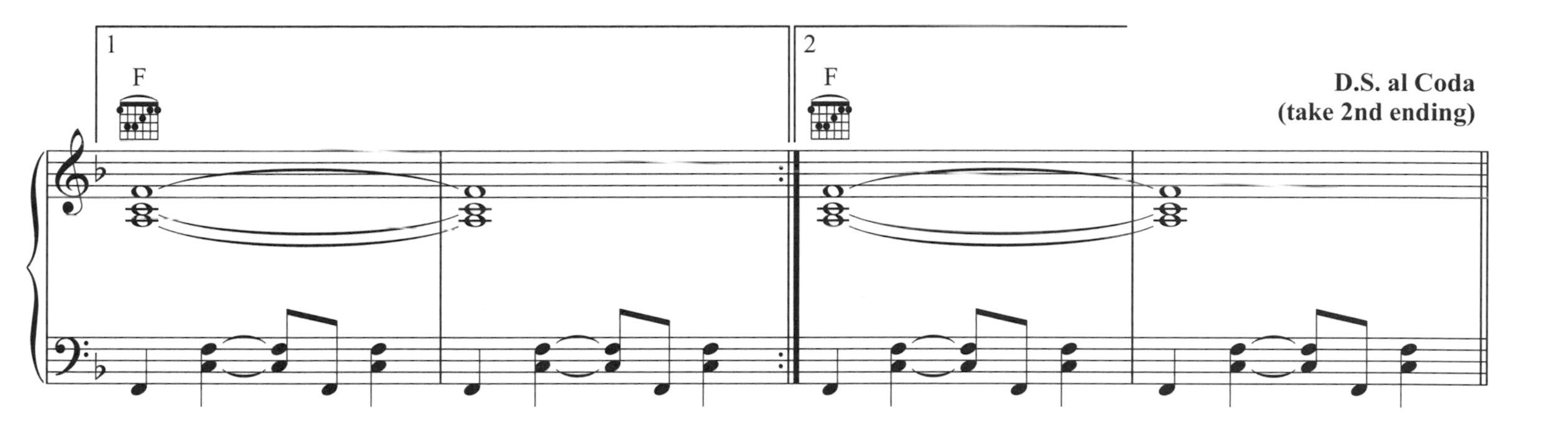
1
F
2
F
D.S. al Coda
(take 2nd ending)

CODA
F
gain.

THE FIREMAN'S TALKIN'

Words and Music by
BOB SEGER

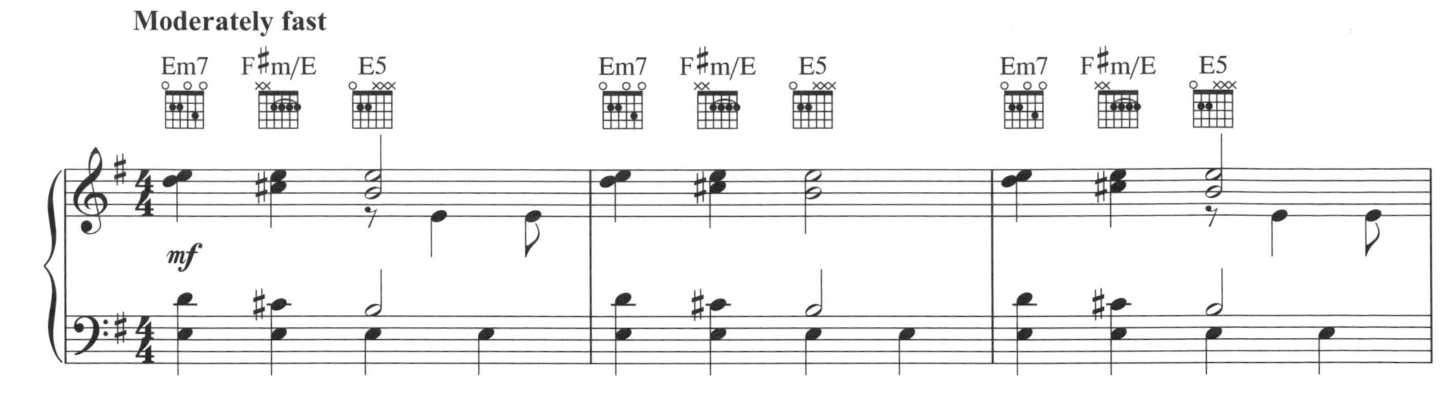

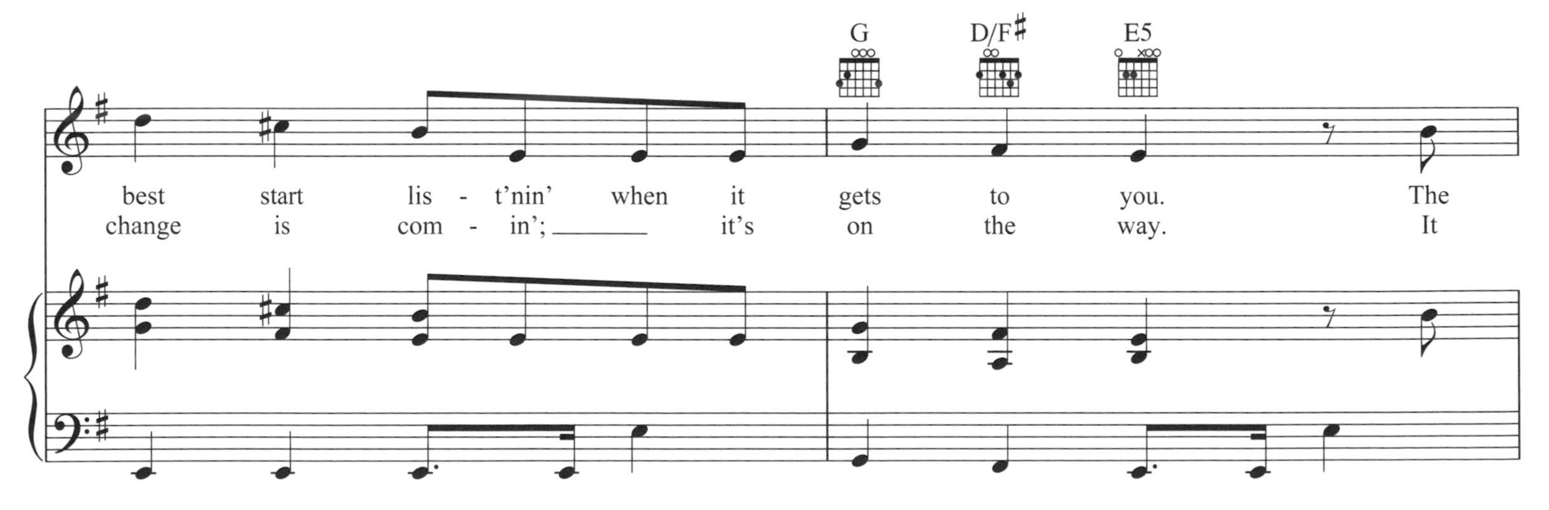

G
D/F♯
E5
1
Gsus2/B
5fr
B7sus
4fr
no more time. You know you're out of
will get here. You
E5
2fr
2
Gsus2
time. There's know it
F♯m7
E5
will get here. You
G
D/F♯
E5
know it will get here.

Bm
A
You will feel it right out - side your
Liv - in' in Or - lan - do by the

E
E5
1
Bm
door.
sea,
You won't be de -

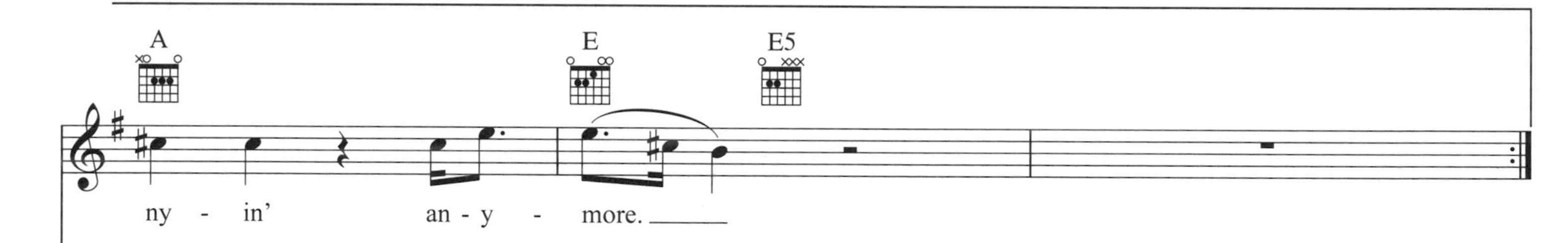
A
E
E5
ny - in' an - y - more.

2
Bm
A
A5
5fr
where will all your mag - ic be? Right where

G5
3fr
D/F♯
E5
it
should
be.

Em7
F♯m/E
E5

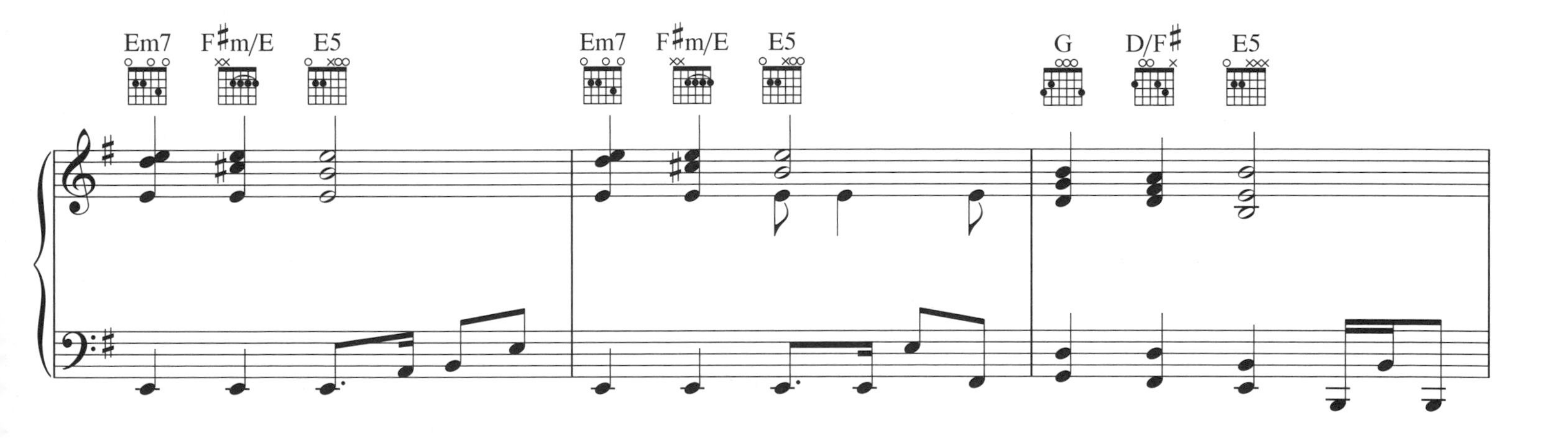
Em7
F♯m/E
E5
Em7
F♯m/E
E5
G
D/F♯
E5

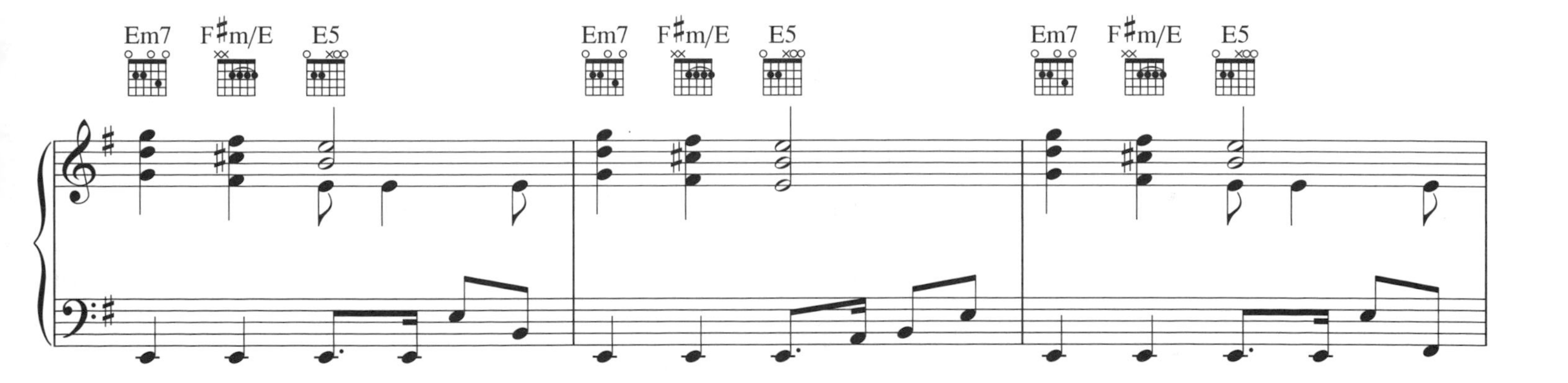
Em7
F♯m/E
E5
Em7
F♯m/E
E5
Em7
F♯m/E
E5

G D/F# Em E5
The fire - man's talk - in'; his words are clear. It
might take dec - ades, but it will get here. There's
G D/F# E5
no more hid - in' the truth a - way. The fire - man's talk - in'; it's
Suddenly slower
G D/F# E5 G(add2) B7sus E5
2fr
on the way, it's on the way.
rit.

LET THE RIVERS RUN

Words and Music by
BOB SEGER

E5
B/E
A/E
al - ways a hill
out there be - yond
reach for the sky,
on - ly to fall.
E5
A5
5fr
E5
where I could be,
and
They nev - er change;
B5
A5
5fr
E5
1
where I be - long.
I've seen them all.
2
A
E
Let the riv - ers run like they
run from the

A E A E
al - ways do. It's not up to me, it's not
Great Di - vide. I will stay with you, I'll be
B5 A5 5fr E5 A
up to you. When we reach the
by your side. When we reach the
E A E
end, when our time is done, let us
end, when our words are done, let us
A E B5 A5 5fr E5
all be still while the riv - ers run.
lis - ten well while the riv - ers run.
To Coda
8vb

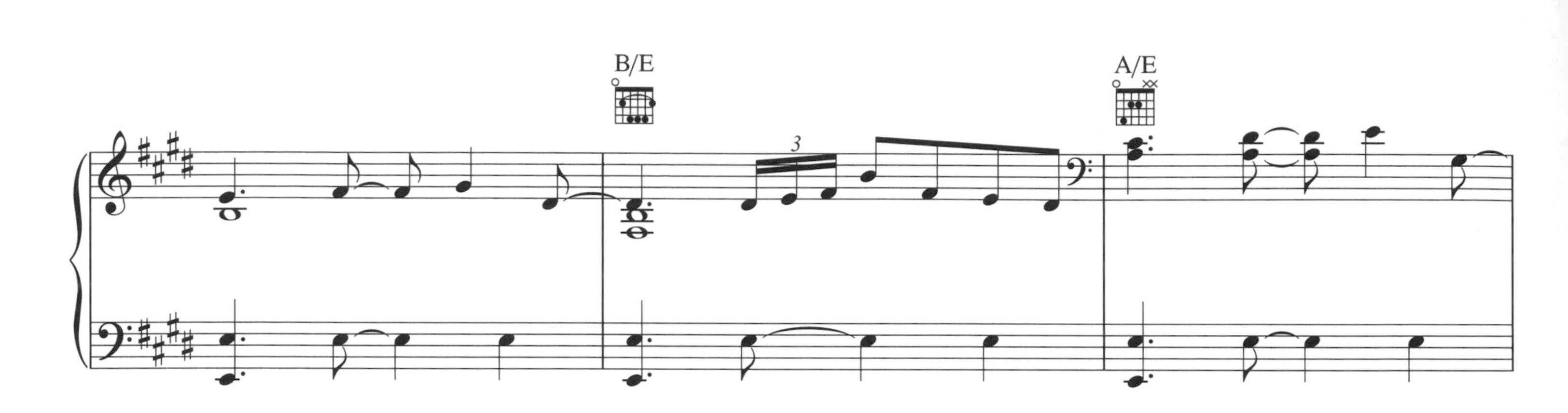
B/E
A/E
3

E
A
E

B
E5

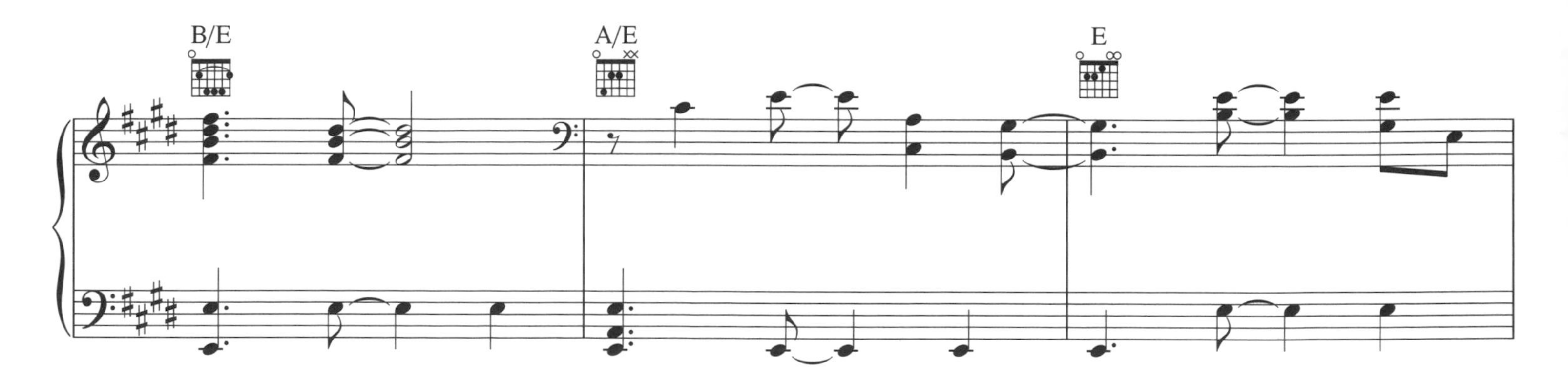
B/E
A/E
E

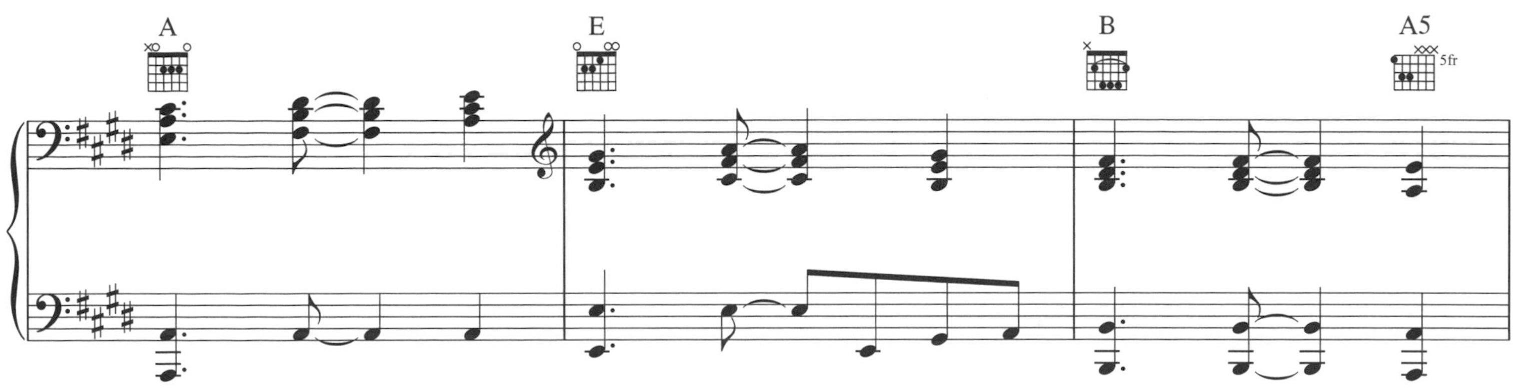
A
E
B
A5
5fr

E5
A
D.S. al Coda
Let the riv - ers
8vb

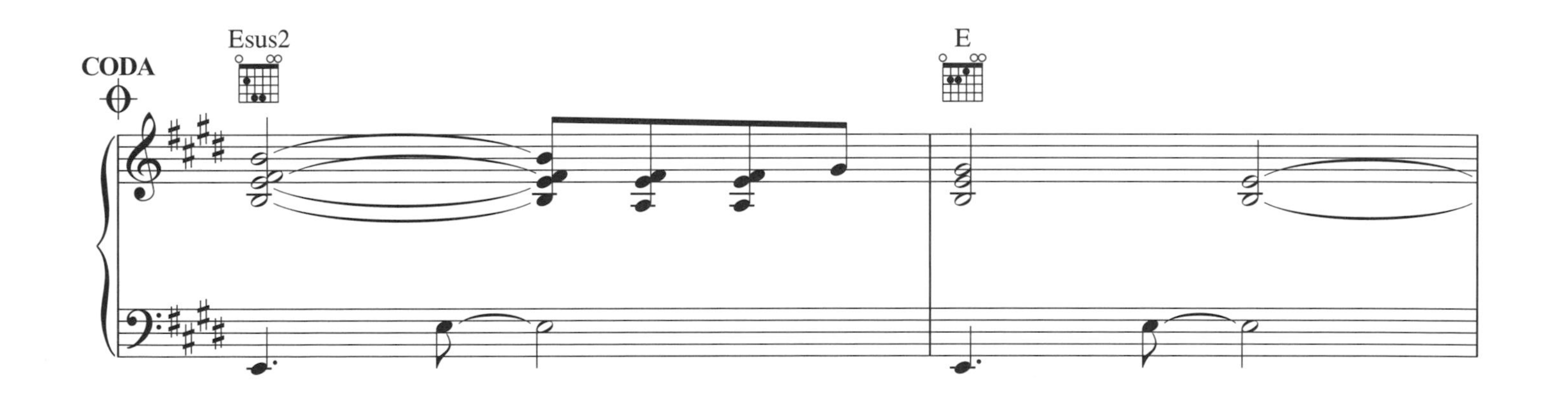
CODA
Esus2
E

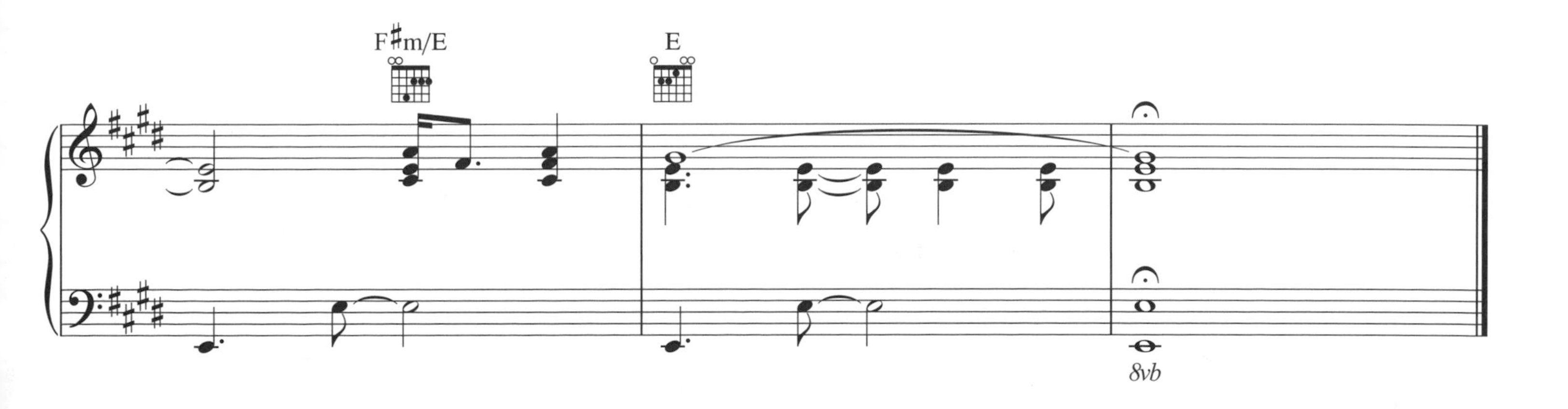
F♯m/E
E
8vb